Reformed Spirituality

to Shin Hwa

with appreciation for our time together as companions on the inner way. May you know the company of the Risen - One on your way.

Howard Rice

3/15/95

REFORMED · SPIRITUALITY

An Introduction for Believers

Howard L. Rice

Westminster/John Knox Press
Louisville, Kentucky

Book design by Gene Harris

First edition

Published by Westminster/John Knox Press
Louisville, Kentucky

PRINTED IN THE UNITED STATES OF AMERICA

9   8   7   6   5   4

Library of Congress Cataloging-in-Publication Data

Rice, Howard L.
   Reformed spirituality : an introduction for believers / Howard L. Rice. — 1st ed.
       p.   cm.
   Includes bibliographical references and index.
   ISBN 0-664-25230-3

   1. Spirituality—Reformed Church.   2. Reformed Church—Doctrines. I. Title.
BV4501.2.R5112 1991
248—dc20   91-15200

To my teachers, especially Frank Cross, Edward Dowey, George M. Gibson, Morton Kelsey, Cecil Lower, Marshall Scott, Mary Elizabeth Thompson, Viola Wendt, George William-Smith, and G. Ernest Wright.

To my students at San Francisco Theological Seminary.

And to my wonderful wife, Nancy, who is my best friend and my partner for life.

Reality, in fact, is always something you couldn't have guessed. That's *one* of the reasons I believe Christianity. It's a religion you couldn't have guessed.

—C. S. Lewis in *The Case for Christianity*

Contents

Foreword

Howard Rice has opened the door to a long-neglected treasury of Reformed spiritual practice. He also provides a balanced, compassionate, and eloquent vision of true Christian maturity. Personal spiritual discipline is placed within the context of the full Christian life where it belongs and in the frame of reference where it was understood in the best of Reformed thinking. The author has written a wise and passionate account of the human encounter and relationship with our God of infinite mystery, wisdom, intelligence, and love. His book is fully documented and yet very readable and religiously nourishing, a wise guide not only to spiritual life but to the full Christian life. The author shares his own struggle and growth, and the book breathes a spirit of compassion, wisdom, and charity.

My religious background was that of the Reformed tradition. I was exposed only to the intellectual and dogmatic side of Calvin, however, and the religious movement that sprang from him. *Reformed Spirituality* opened my eyes to an aspect of Reformed Christian life of which I had not been aware. I began to see that there was a spiritual dimension to this movement that resulted not only in the writing of Calvin, but in the words of John Bunyan, Jonathan Edwards, and numerous other writers right up to our own century. This book provides a discussion of many of these writers and also quotes large sections of their prayers and spiritual writings.

Reformed Spirituality is a mine of rich religious ore. What puzzled me most as I read Rice's book was how this rich tradition was largely lost or neglected within the Reformed churches, and totally ignored and overlooked by writers outside that tradition interested in the spiritual life. Rice shows how and why this suspicion of private spiritual practice developed. His work is a breakthrough study of the rich and varied spiritual resources within the Reformed tradition which had been almost entirely lost.

So often we see only what we are looking for. This is true of most of our reading, whether secular reading or reading of the Bible, the church Fathers, and John Calvin. The subject of healing and ecstatic experience in dreams, visions, or other encounters with the holy in the Bible and in the history of the church have been largely ignored or ridiculed by most modern religious writers. The author knows well the most significant writings of John Calvin, and he quotes passages that show a very different picture of Calvin from the popular one. The word "spiritual," or "spirituality," was not often used in Reformed writing. The word "piety" covered much the same ground and has much the same meaning as our current word "spirituality."

Calvin emphasized the need for times of private prayer and quietness alone with God. His method of Bible-reading is very close to the meditative method of the Benedictines, known as the *lectio divina.* He believed that human beings could find forgiveness and guidance from God in their private prayer times, but he also recognized the uniqueness of human beings and knew that some people needed the guidance and direction of the pastor or a mature member of the congregation. Calvin gives profound suggestions for spiritual guidance or companionship. Both Calvin and those who followed him advocated the practice of keeping a journal of one's religious life, and many of these journals have come down to us. Although the covenant groups of the Reformed movement were not as central as the small-group fellowship in the Methodist Church, they were encouraged as a way of spiritual and ethical growth. Calvin stated that we human beings need not only our private prayer and Bible-reading, but also the fellowship of public worship. He placed great value on the Eucharist and believed that people came to a mystical communion with Christ in that sacrament. He also stated, as do all the best spiritual writers, that a spiritual life that does not issue forth in works of love to those close and those distant, and in social justice, is not true spirituality. For Calvin, religion and government could not be separated. Many Calvinist ideas about government and the rights of individuals have been embodied in the Declaration of Independence and in the Constitution of the United States.

This interest in the spiritual life did not cease with Calvin. John Bunyan's *Pilgrim's Progress* expresses the basic vision of the Reformed life-style in allegory and images. This book was a close second to the Bible in the lives of many Protestants for centuries. M. Esther Harding has written a fascinating psychological study of *Pilgrim's Progress* in her book *Journey Into Self.* She states that Bunyan provides an excellent description of the way to psychological wholeness and integration. One of the greatest of American theologians, Jonathan Edwards, writing during the Great Awakening, struggled with the problem of integrating the reality of religious experience and sound theology. Many other profound discussions of the spiritual life flowed from the Reformed movement and are quoted in the text that follows.

The Puritans left their homes and journeyed to a strange land to have the freedom to follow the basic ideas and practices of the Reformed movement. Any religious movement that could ignite spiritual fire in religious seekers in Europe and then become the dominant point of view in the New World and spread, as it has, throughout our globe, has real depth and power. Howard Rice reveals one reason that this religious message touched so many men and women. Some people have viewed the Puritans and their followers as dour, but they faced the fact that though their religious way was a difficult one, it was one that provided infinite existential meaning and satisfaction. The full Reformed tradition, like Calvin, deals with the complexities and mystery of human existence; and it provides for both stringent thinking and the rich life of feelings, emotions, and the direct experience of God. It encourages many different ways of approaching God.

This book can open the eyes of most people in the Reformed tradition to the depth, wisdom, and wealth of their spiritual tradition. It can also guide any Christian, Protestant or Catholic, to a more profound and holistic understanding of the full spiritual life, both in the inner dimension of that life, in the necessity for communal religious experience, and in the importance of social and political commitment and action. In the process we can learn to appreciate another great Christian, John Calvin. *Reformed Spirituality* deserves a large and wide readership.

MORTON KELSEY

Acknowledgments

I am deeply indebted to Dr. Roy Fairchild, long a colleague at San Francisco Theological Seminary, whose work in the field of Christian spirituality from a Reformed perspective has stimulated and nourished me. No words are adequate to express my debt to Professor Morton Kelsey who, though an Anglican himself, has encouraged me to do this exploration into my own tradition. I am deeply grateful for the influence of Dr. Kelsey, whose ideas have planted many seeds in me of which this book is the fruit. His profound insights can be recognized throughout the manuscript. I also owe much to the Reverend Kenneth Meece, a former student who first introduced me to the work of Morton Kelsey and to the practice of meditation. I am grateful for the kindness of my students at San Francisco Theological Seminary. Debra Baker and Steven Doriss read the manuscript and offered significant suggestions for change and improvement. Kathy Makus was a great help in editing the manuscript. She is responsible for the accuracy of the citations. As a teacher, I continue to celebrate what I keep learning from my students!

My wife, Nancy, kept me going at times when I might well have given up. She regularly suggested, "Just work at it one hour today!" Those hours added up. Barbara Hiatt, my friend and colleague, was a tremendous help by attending to details that otherwise would have eroded my time and energy.

The Board of Trustees of San Francisco Theological Seminary gave me a very generous twelve-month sabbatical leave, and the time was essential for the completion of this book. The ideas had been in my head and heart for years. The pastors of the Presbytery of Santa Barbara meeting for a retreat and those pastors who attended a midwinter Nebraska pastors' conference at Hastings College were kind enough to provide opportunity for me to test this material and to offer helpful suggestions. Although I had lectured repeatedly on the subjects covered in this manuscript, I needed time to get the material into shape for publication, and that was a more massive task than I had anticipated. Without the sabbatical leave, it would never have been finished.

H. L. R.

Reformed Spirituality:
An Introduction

Q. What is your only comfort in life and in death?
A. That I belong—body and soul, in life and in death—not to myself but to my faithful Savior, Jesus Christ, who at the cost of his own blood has fully paid for all my sins and has completely freed me from the dominion of the devil; that he protects me so well that without the will of my Father in heaven not a hair can fall from my head; indeed, that everything must fit his purpose for my salvation. Therefore, by his Holy Spirit, he also assures me of eternal life, and makes me wholeheartedly willing and ready from now on to live for him.

The Heidelberg Catechism[1]

The longing for direct, firsthand experience is the source of the tremendous interest on the part of Protestants in the mainstream denominations in the subject of spirituality. Books on prayer and the inner life have been increasingly popular for over a decade, and small groups, often without benefit of clergy, gather to share their experiences of God's presence in their lives.

One of the major causes of the search for religious experience is a sense that modern life has become flat and without passion or a sense of purpose. Furthermore, religion is frequently reduced to a rather boring set of ritual acts and duties which may have little impact on a person's sense of God's presence or leading.

There are many people for whom ordinary religious practices are not sufficient. They seek a deeper experiential relationship with God and a faith that is grounded in "firsthand" knowing. These people are hungry for something more than formal religious activities. Some of the most sensitive of such seekers have left institutional religion altogether in their search for something that can be sensed in the heart as well as known in the mind. Their searching has created a demand which has been filled by "pop" movements that abound today. The same quest is behind the interest in Eastern religion and in what is called "new age" religion. In somewhat different forms, it is responsible for the increase in the number and popularity of a variety of cults.

The heart of the Christian life is the deeply confident affirmation of experiential faith in a God who cares and who can be relied on to continue to care when all else seems to be lost or in serious question. The Heidelberg Catechism, which is structured to deal with three principal themes of the Christian life—guilt, grace, and gratitude[2]—expresses this central tenet of Christian faith in terms of its being our "only comfort," because in the midst of a world of uncertainty and confusion the assurance of God's unfailing love keeps us from helplessness or despair. Because of what God has done for us, we are able to respond in our desire to live with and for this loving God. The whole of the Christian life is response to God's gracious initiative. We live gratefully both in the private and internal relationship we have with God and in the more public and corporate expressions of faith.

The deliberate effort to assist Christians with the process of intentional cultivation of a sense of God's presence in their lives has become a significant movement in recent years. It has placed an emphasis on the ways by which we open ourselves to the presence of God and has spread widely among Christians of different denominational traditions, racial ethnic backgrounds, and theological points of view. It is having a profound impact on pastors and people, congregations, seminaries, and denominational structures. It is a movement that appears to be growing from the ground up: The people in the pew are expressing their interest. Pastors then respond and seek assistance from hesitant and frequently unprepared governing bodies and seminaries.

Although this wave of interest in meditation, the practice of silence, reflective reading of scripture, and finding a spiritual companion or director is common among Christians of all denominational traditions, the Protestant churches have often turned a deaf ear to the need expressed by those who are seeking this form of spiritual assistance for their lives. There is a particularly deeply embedded resistance to spirituality among those churches within the denominational tradition called Reformed.

The Reformed tradition embraces those Protestant denominations which trace their roots to the Swiss Reformation in the sixteenth century led by Huldrych Zwingli in Zurich, from approximately 1523 until his death in 1531, and by John Calvin in Geneva, from 1536 until his death in 1564. These churches, which generally call themselves Reformed if they originated on the continent of Europe and Presbyterian if they began in the British Isles, share some common characteristics. With the exception of the Hungarian Reformed Churches, which have always had bishops, they nearly always have a form of government that is representative and vests power in governing bodies rather than in individuals. They tend to be suspicious of formalism in worship and emphasize the centrality of scripture and the sermon. They frequently see the rigorous exercise of the intellect as a sign of obedience to God. They have always been concerned to address the needs of society by applying the gospel to the issues of the world. The denominations in the United States usually considered to be part of the Reformed tradition include the Presbyterians, the United Church of Christ, the Reformed Church in America, the Christian Reformed Church, and, though it can be debated, the Disciples of Christ. There are, in addition, persons strongly influenced by the Reformed tradition within the Baptist, Methodist, and Anglican traditions.

No one can be part of a church within this tradition for very long without meeting the suspicion that seem to be aroused by the subject of spirituality. This resistance is the probable result of several factors, not least of them a lack of appreciation of their own tradition itself. Although most Reformed Protestants recognize the centrality of the scriptures for their faith, and many appreciate the importance of considered response to issues in the world, most Reformed Christians are quite unaware that they are a part of a living tradition that has much to contribute to the world church in the area of the spiritual life. Most of the books recently written on the subject of spirituality do not help, and by omission of any Reformed sources they reinforce the idea that the Reformed tradition is somehow lacking in this dimension of its life.

Because Reformed Protestants do not recognize and are not taught that there is a spiritual tradition within their own heritage, they have frequently had no basis to integrate their own experience into their faith or church life. They have been hesitant even to speak about their religious experiences for fear of being ridiculed or rejected. They may have dropped out of the organized church completely to become part of the "believing without belonging" subculture.

This book is an effort to reclaim that part of the heritage of the Reformed tradition which provides guidance for the development of a living sense of the present reality of God. This heritage properly belongs to every Reformed Christian, and without it we are impoverished in our Christian lives, weakened in the struggle to be faithful in the world, and wearied by the effort to live with integrity. Reformed Christians have a healthy spiritual tradition to share with other Christians, which it is possible to identify. I believe that the recovery of the spiritual tradition among people within the Reformed tradition will enable us to offer strength to the whole church. It is my hope that by strengthening the faith and witness of one part of the body of Christ, the whole church can be helped.

Sources from the Sixteenth Century

In order to begin this task, I have found it necessary to go back to the beginning, to reconsider the work of John Calvin. Reformed Christians have continued to find inspiration for their faith in the writing of this brilliant pastor and theologian. He has frequently been interpreted as a scholarly intellectual who had little interest in personal piety. An examination of his most important work, the *Institutes of the Christian Religion,* his commentaries, and his letters enables one to discover that Calvin's primary purpose throughout everything he wrote was to assist the believer in the struggle to live faithfully as one who knows Christ and is in the process of coming into union with Christ. Calvin thus saw the life of faith as a unity in both its outer and its inner expressions.

Three Reformed confessional documents from the sixteenth century have continued to exercise great influence upon people of different denominations and nations throughout the centuries. The oldest is the Scots Confession (1560). This confession is also the first to have been written in the English language. The Scottish Parliament, after a bloody civil war, invited John Knox and five other leaders of the Reformation to draft this confession for use by the church and nation. The work was completed in only four days, and it still bears the marks of the haste of its authors. It also shows the scars of the violent period of its authorship and the intensity of feelings, especially anti-Catholic sentiments, that were the products of the costly and bitter war.

The second confessional document is the Heidelberg Catechism of 1563 which was drafted by two persons, Caspar Olevianus and Zacharias Ursinus, at the request of Elector Frederick III of the Palatinate in Germany. It was an effort to clarify the Reformed faith over against both

Roman Catholic teaching and orthodox Lutheran teaching. Reformed Protestants were caught between these two more powerful movements in Germany and needed something to sustain them in persecution. The Heidelberg Catechism is a personal document which still brings strength and hope to the reader.

The Second Helvetic Confession, written by Heinrich Bullinger, Zwingli's successor in Zurich, was not very well known until 1966 when a new English translation was published to celebrate the four hundredth anniversary of its writing. It is included in the Presbyterian *Book of Confessions* and, in spite of the heated spirit of the time and hostility toward the Church of Rome, it has an amazingly reconciling and ecumenical spirit. It places an emphasis on the need for a deep relationship with God. Because it is the longest Reformed confession, it has the most well-developed doctrine of the church, and it includes a discussion of the various spiritual disciplines of fasting, prayer, chastity, and the sacraments.

British Puritans and Presbyterians
of the Seventeenth Century

I have also concentrated on the Puritans as the heirs of Calvin in both theology and practice. Puritanism was the British manifestation of continental Pietism, and as such it was also a protest against religious formalism, dogmatism, and lack of passion. The Puritans took their lively sense of a relationship with God seriously, and it led them to seek to purify the Church of England and also to reform the government of the nation. Following the overthrow of the monarchy during the English Civil War, the Puritan-dominated Parliament controlled the government. The Westminster Assembly was called by Parliament for the purpose of drafting a new confession of faith, form of government, and form of worship for the Church of England. That assembly met over a period of years, concluding its work in 1647. One of the reasons for the length of the Westminster Assembly was the need to resolve differences between presbyterian Puritans, who believed in vesting power in structures beyond the congregation, and congregational Puritans, who saw the congregation as the single source of unity and power and wished no interference with the autonomy of the congregation. The irony of that Assembly is that the restoration of the crown to Charles II also produced a return to the episcopacy of the Church of England, and the documents produced by the Assembly were officially adopted by the Church of Scotland and ignored in the Church of England.

The Westminster Confession of Faith and the Westminster Larger and Shorter Catechisms are the best-known confessions among English-speaking Presbyterians and those most deeply affected by them, for example, Presbyterians in Mexico, Korea, Nigeria, and Kenya, where missionaries from Scotland, England, and the United States carried these confessional documents with them.

In the United States the Westminster Confession was first adopted by the Congregational Synod of the Massachusetts Bay Colony in 1648, after having been modified to affirm congregational church polity. The first synod of the Presbyterian Church in the American colonies adopted the Westminster documents in 1729. The Philadelphia Confession of Faith, an adaptation of the Westminster Confession of Faith modified to affirm congregational polity and baptism of believers, was adopted by the American Baptists in 1742.[3] It has continued to exert a powerful influence on the theology and piety of American Protestants.

Among the contributions of the Puritans, I have paid special attention to *The Practice of Piety,* by Lewis Bayly, a Puritan who remained within the Church of England. This book was one of the most influential of all the multitude of guides for the spiritual life published by and for Puritans. The date of its first publication is not known, but by 1613 it had reached its third edition, and by 1735 a fifty-ninth edition was published. It was translated into Welsh, Polish, German, and French. In 1665, the Puritans of New England published a translation for Native Americans in Massachusetts.

I have also used the writing of a Puritan mystic whose work is relatively unknown today. Francis Rous (1579– 1659) began as a Presbyterian and later moved toward an Independent (Congregational) Puritan position. He was the speaker of the House of Commons during the period of the Commonwealth and was a model of the Puritan ideal of the theologically articulate layperson. He served as a lay member of the Westminster Assembly for a time. His essay, "The Mystical Marriage," is a splendid example of Puritan mystical theology which did not hesitate to borrow from and adapt medieval sources. Like Calvin, Rous was strongly influenced by fourteenth-century bridal mysticism.[4] Like John of the Cross, he maintained that spiritual marriage of the soul to God is not achieved in this life, but only betrothal.

A particularly significant Scottish Presbyterian figure of the same period is Samuel Rutherford (1600–1661), who was also a participant in the Westminster Assembly. It was Rutherford's normal practice to begin his day at three A.M., with meditation and prayers. He was outspoken in his opposition to episcopacy, and in 1636 published a theological treatise that incurred the wrath of the bishop of Galloway. He was forbidden to exercise his ministry and ordered to reside in Aberdeen in exile for eighteen months. During that time, he wrote many letters, which were collected, edited, and published in 1674 after his death. These letters of advice reveal his own inner thoughts and spiritual practices. They demonstrate the centrality of experiential faith for him. He was later able to return to his parish and was a commissioner at the General Assembly of 1638. He was appointed as a commissioner to the Westminster Assembly from the Church of Scotland in 1643 and served four years.

Richard Baxter (1615–1691) is perhaps the most prolific and well known of the English Puritan writers. He was, for a time, a chaplain in Oliver Cromwell's army. During the period after the restoration of the monarchy, when Puritanism became less political and more inward, he shared with other Puritans intense interest in the question, How do I know if I am saved? Having lost their effort to lead a new Reformation in England, Puritans began to seek consolation and assurance rather than power. Baxter led the effort to reformulate Puritan life and thought in a post-Puritan world. His solution to the question of identity and security of salvation was that the answer was to be found in meditation. Baxter was deeply interested in the subjects of prayer and meditation and utilized the Benedictine method of *lectio divina* as a Reformed method of reflection and meditation upon scripture. A devout Calvinist, he sought to provide guidance to pastors in their work as spiritual guides and can be said to have adapted a Reformed method of spiritual guidance.

John Owen (1616–1683) was probably the greatest scholar of Puritanism. He was the dean of Christ Church, Oxford, and the vice-chancellor of Oxford University, and Cromwell's chaplain in Ireland. He has been called the Calvin of England because his writings are both thoroughly academic and completely relevant to the life of the believer.

John Bunyan (1628–1688), the poet and rebel who was a self-educated itinerant preacher, is remembered for *Pilgrim's Progress,* the most widely influential book among Puritans and their heirs for well over a century. Much of the imagery of Puritan devotion came from this single book which, along with the Bible, was to be found in nearly every Puritan home.

Henry Scougal (1650–1678) was a Scottish Calvinist Episcopalian whose single book, *The Life of God in the Soul of Man,* was another very influential resource among Scottish Presbyterians and English and American Puritans.

Eighteenth-Century Calvinists

Elizabeth Singer Rowe (1647–1737) was the first widely read Protestant woman in England. The daughter of a Protestant, non-Anglican minister and educated religiously, she nevertheless wrote books of secular poetry, her first under the pen name of "Philomela" in 1696. Only after the death of her husband did she retire to a life of spiritual retreat. After her death, her close friend Isaac Watts, following her directions, revised and published a collection of her prayers which he called *The Devout Exercises of the Heart.* It was widely circulated and published in many editions and in many languages.

Gerhard Tersteegen (1697–1769) was a Dutch Calvinist, best known for his hymns. Unfortunately, most of his writing has not been translated into English. His strongly mystical bent was deeply biblical in orientation and was an excellent example of Dutch Calvinist pietism. Because pietism was a protest against rigid orthodoxy, it became highly influential across the English Channel.

Jonathan Edwards (1703–1758) was one of the first, and many would say the greatest, of American theologians. He sought to revitalize orthodox Calvinism, which had degenerated into a religion of static intellectual propositions. Edwards' goal was to make Calvinism relevant to the social setting of the time. He "attempted to recapture the living experience of God in Christ which had once informed Puritanism."[5] His impact was felt most directly through his association with the Great Awakening. This movement, for spiritual renewal of a faith that could be felt as well as thought, took place during the 1740s in his own congregation in Northampton, Massachusetts. Edwards tried to distinguish, in the passion of the highly emotional experiences of conversion among his own parishioners, between what he saw as spurious conversions and genuine ones. In so doing, he developed a solid foundation for spiritual discernment. He fought against excessive reliance on the conversion experience itself, because it could be produced by human effort. Edwards sought to keep God's providence central, yet saw the significance of the new emphasis on the conversion experience as an important sign of God's work among the people.

Nineteenth- and Twentieth-Century Figures

Charles Hodge (1789–1878), the primary representative of orthodox Calvinism, or Princeton theology as it was called, was also a man of intense personal faith. His book *The Way of Life* is an excellent example of guidance on prayer, meditation, and the practice of other spiritual disciplines. It shows that even among the most orthodox Calvinists, there remained a deeply personal and experiential faith.

Emily Herman (1876–1923) was the wife of a Presbyterian minister. She spent much of her early life in Constantinople and Sydney. In 1908 she began her work as a journalist, and in 1913 was appointed editor of the publication of the Presbyterian Church of England, *The Presbyterian*. Toward the end of her life she joined the Church of England. She was the author of many books on prayer and the spiritual life, frequently debating with Evelyn Underhill, her far-better-known contemporary.

Howard Thurman (1899–1981) was really not within the denominational limits of the Reformed tradition. He was an ecumenical Christian who can only be classified as Reformed by the quality of his writings and the character of his spirituality. His extensive research and literary output are amazing. He explored the relationship between the inner life and social justice, and was among the first American writers to develop the principle of nonviolent resistance. He was especially influential in the cause of civil rights because of his deep impact on Dr. Martin Luther King, Jr.

Summary of Sources

These are the most important primary sources from which I have drawn. They share a common set of assumptions about the spiritual life and are all, in some way, heirs to the Genevan Reformation. I hope to show their common themes and to demonstrate that there is something that can be called a "Reformed spiritual tradition." Other authors are drawn on throughout this book, and I refer the reader to the Bibliography for a complete listing of the works used and cited.

Although most of my references are from writers within

the Reformed tradition, there is no way to be properly Reformed without an ecumenical appreciation for the work of all those parts of the church universal which share in the task of helping to give guidance and direction for the shape of the Christian life. Calvin was never reluctant to quote from Roman Catholic sources, and his heirs in Puritanism frequently used the medieval devotional classics. The Reformed tradition is one that has, from the beginning, sought to be ecumenical. I have deliberately limited myself in order to demonstrate to the reader the breadth and scope of thought available within the Reformed tradition itself. I regret that time and lack of adequate bibliographic resources have limited me to writers from North America and Europe, and I believe that an important future task is to discover and appreciate the work of Third World Reformed Christians.

The ongoing motto of the Reformed tradition, "The church reformed, always being reformed," strongly suggests that to be truly reformed is not to get stuck in the sixteenth or any other century. In each age, God calls people to be faithful in the context in which they live. We do not have to be against everything that the Reformers, in their life-and-death struggle against the might of the papacy, rejected. Indeed, in this post–Vatican II ecumenical era we may be able to reconsider such practices as silent retreats, kneeling for prayer, making the sign of the cross, and the use of icons. These have been rejected by most Protestants until recently, not because they were unbiblical or sub-Christian, but because our forebears threw them out as remnants of Roman Catholic piety.

The book begins with the issue of the role of experience in the life of the Christian as it has been interpreted in the Reformed tradition. Because Reformed Christians have often seemed almost afraid of their experiences, it is important to provide a corrective to the unnecessarily negative connotations that accompany the idea of religious experience.

Chapter 2 is an interpretation of the principal causes of the resistance to spirituality which seems so deeply ingrained among many Reformed Protestants. It seeks to explore beyond those misconceptions of the tradition of Christian spirituality which are the basis for suspicions about anything connected to the practice of spirituality. It also seeks to explore possibilities for moving forward, in faithfulness to the tradition, integrating a particularly Reformed spirituality into the lives of persons who are seeking for such guidance and grounding today.

The four chapters that follow seek to explore four essential areas of Christian spirituality for which the Reformed tradition provides guidance: prayer, devotional study of scripture, spiritual guidance, and work for justice and peace in the world.

The last chapter seeks to be of assistance to the Christian aiming to explore the practice of spirituality. It is necessary to examine, first, the role of discipline in the spiritual life, and then to see that life as a pilgrimage in which there are ups and downs, times of reassurance and times of doubt. No one should venture into spiritual depths without being forewarned of the dangers and pitfalls ahead, and without being prepared for the wonderful surprises as well.

NOTES

1. Presbyterian Church (U.S.A.), *The Book of Confessions* (New York and Atlanta: Office of the General Assembly, 1983), 4.001.
2. Jack Rogers, *Presbyterian Creeds: A Guide to the Book of Confessions* (Philadelphia: Westminster Press, 1985), p. 108.
3. Rogers, *Presbyterian Creeds,* p. 141.
4. Urban T. Holmes, *A History of Christian Spirituality* (New York: Seabury Press, 1980), p. 131.
5. John Dillenberger and Claude Welch, *Protestant Christianity* (New York: Charles Scribner's Sons, 1954), p. 137.

1

The Experience of God in the Reformed Tradition

Our faith and its assurance do not proceed from flesh and blood, that is to say, from natural powers within us, but are the inspiration of the Holy Ghost; whom we confess to be God, equal with the Father and with his Son, who sanctifies us, and brings us into all truth by his own working, without whom we should remain forever enemies to God and ignorant of his son, Christ Jesus. For by nature we are so dead, blind, and perverse, that neither can we feel when we are pricked, see the light when it shines, nor assent to the will of God when it is revealed, unless the Spirit of the Lord Jesus quicken that which is dead, remove the darkness from our minds, and bow our stubborn hearts to the obedience of his blessed will.

The Scots Confession[1]

Central to the intensity of contemporary interest in the spiritual life is the desire for personal religious experience. Many people have become serious in their search for a living and vital relationship with God because they feel empty. In a confusing world, in which there seems to be very little that one can trust, many people seek the certainty of God's nearness and reliability which only a direct sense of God's presence can bring.

The desire for personal experience of God is not new or

unique to our particular time in history. Long ago, the
psalmist declared:

> As a deer longs for flowing streams,
>   so my soul longs for you, O God.
> My soul thirsts for God,
>   for the living God.
>
> (Ps. 42:1–2a)

To be human is to be created for relationship with God,
and anything other than such a relationship leaves us
unsatisfied, even when we cannot name what we want.
Human restlessness is one form that the longing for God
takes; it urges us on and prods us. Until we discover that
God is real for us, we are likely to continue to be dissatisfied
and unfulfilled.

There is something about being human that leads us to
want more than we have, to be dissatisfied even when we
obtain those things which we want very much. When we
achieve a particular goal, there is still a hollowness within.
The empty feeling will not be satisfied by possessions,
prestige, power, or money, because it is rooted in our very
human nature. Saint Augustine's words remain true for all
people in all times: "Thou awakest us to delight in Thy
praise; for Thou madest us for Thyself, and our heart is
restless, until it repose in Thee."[2]

The experience of God's closeness is a blessing and a
source of courage, but it is also a source of discomfort.
People frequently try to avoid, or hide from, any direct
sense of God. People may, in fact, be frightened about
having direct experience of God. They may be appropriate-
ly anxious about the consequences of such experience, but
such escape is never completely successful because though
our sense of God's reality and presence, as Calvin claims,
"may sometimes seem to vanish for a moment, it returns at
once and rushes in with new force. If for these there is any
respite from anxiety of conscience, it is not much different
from the sleep of drunken or frenzied persons, who do not
rest peacefully even while sleeping because they are continually troubled with dire and dreadful dreams. The impious

themselves therefore exemplify the fact that some conception of God is ever alive in all men's minds."[3] This seeking God will not let us go. Escape from God may take many forms: busyness, noise, even active participation in the church, which enables us to believe that we are being religious when, in fact, the activity of the organization may keep us at arm's distance from the real God.

So long as life is reasonably satisfactory, the need for God can be ignored. There are thousands of ways of keeping so busy that we can pretend that we are fulfilled in spite of the emptiness. In the state of contentment, there is no desire for change and, because of a common intuition that God may demand change from those who get close enough, there is no real desire for intimacy with God.

The moments of complete contentment are generally brief, and they are interspersed with times of hurt, doubt, pain, and confusion. We are haunted by memories that will not go away and face situations in which everything we had relied on falls apart. A loved one dies, and we do not know whether we can carry on. Age or illness robs us of energy and the ability to accomplish something that we had set out to achieve. A job is taken away by retirement or automation, and only then do we realize how much of ourselves we had invested and how little of ourselves is left apart from the work. A marriage has lost its joy, and we are enduring our time together out of a grim sense of duty or facing the possibility of shattering the dream of a lifetime commitment. A child in whom we have invested great hopes and plans does not turn out as we had expected, and we are shocked, shamed, and bewildered.

The desire for experience of God is rooted in these tragic events, when life is deeply disappointing. When one's inner resources are dried up or insufficient, calling out to God is an act of desperation. When the courage to carry on is just not there, people discover that despair may contain the possibility for being open to God. In the experience of being shattered, human defenses against God are weakened.

Most people who live in the twentieth century have very

strong defenses that form a shield against the experience of God. Perhaps the most impenetrable defense is the mindset that believes only that which the five senses can record. This mind-set limits us to experiences that fit into the narrow range of sense experience. Anything that does not fit into the space-time range is dismissed as nonsense or ignored. This self-imposed boundary means that twentieth-century people are limited in what they are open to acknowledge within their own experience.

Any experience of God's reality requires that some preconceptions be put aside. When we can admit that there is more to the world than sense experience, then we open ourselves to the possibility of being surprised by God. There can be a place for mystery without the need to explain it away or solve it as a puzzle. Experiences of pain and loss are doorways to the sacred, because they force people to let go of their defenses. Once our worldview is disturbed, we can be open to accept experiences that had previously been either ignored or denied.

Morton Kelsey describes how the shallowness of being limited to the material world cannot satisfy "the deepest desires of men and women for transcendence and meaning. People are desperate to discover what it is that makes life worth living, and if they cannot find a healthy way to come into relationship with spiritual reality, then they may seek an unhealthy way to enter the inner world."[4] Some of that unhealthy seeking is going on in our society today because the church has paid too little attention to this basic human longing and frequently belittled people's experiences when they have discovered the courage to speak about them. Instead of castigating the New Age movement, for example, the church needs to question what is missing from its own life that is causing people to gravitate toward such a movement in such large numbers.

From its inception, the Reformed tradition has been highly ambivalent about the role of experience in the Christian life. William Bouwsma, in his biography of Calvin, concludes that Calvin was a highly complex man who can be read in either of two very different ways. The first is that of Calvin as a man of fixed principles who stood in the tradition of the scholasticism of the Middle Ages. "For this Calvin, Christianity tended toward static orthodoxy, and a Christian was a person endowed with certain status."[5] Those who have emphasized this side of Calvin have concluded that to be a Calvinist is to crave order and rationality above all. They have devised a scholastic orthodoxy which allows little room for ambiguity and have been suspicious of any human experience, especially if it does not fit their frame of reference. Although such Reformed voices, and they are many, have frequently spoken about prayer and the Christian life, they have left little room for mystery except for the feeling of fear or awe before the majesty of God. This form of orthodox Calvinism is dramatically expressed in the Westminster Shorter Catechism's definition of God: "God is a Spirit, infinite, eternal, and unchangeable, in his being, wisdom, power, holiness, justice, goodness, and truth."[6] The God so defined hardly inspires a desire for relationship. The static quality of God seems to make prayer pointless, and the complete separation of God from everything human seems to establish a gulf between us that makes God inaccessible to us. The God of scripture—who cries, mourns, is jealous, suffers with the people, whose will can be changed—is at odds with this static description. The changeless God of such Calvinism has been inhospitable to any form of mysticism and uncomfortable with the language of religious experience.

The other side of Calvin celebrated the paradoxes of life, refused to rationalize ambiguity, and welcomed mystery at the heart of the faith. Bouwsma declares that Calvin "also asserted the primacy of experience and practice over theory, and he had a considerable tolerance for individual freedom."[7] For this side of Calvin, the Christian faith had a dynamic character and could not be understood fully. A Christian was a person who was engaged in a lifelong process of growth toward the fullness of Christ. Those who have chosen to emphasize this side of Calvin have come to a very different form of Calvinism. They have been more interested in the quality of faith and life than in the

correctness of doctrine. Because of the less-rigid stance of
this form of Calvinism, it has included a wide range of
different points of view, including the continental pietists,
English and American Puritans, preachers of the Great
Awakening in America, nineteenth-century liberals,
charismatics, evangelicals, and contemporary feminists.
These persons have resisted orthodox formulations, not
because they did not believe these things but because they
wanted freedom for expression of the actual experience of
living people. Among them there has been room for the
mystical and for the mysterious, for a God whose dependa-
bility comes not from being unchangeable but from being
loving. They have not been afraid to celebrate difference
and have pointed to the Christian life as a life lived in the
company of Christ. Frequently these Calvinists have borrowed from the language of medieval mysticism to try to
describe their own experiences.

Because both forms of the Reformed tradition are rooted
in one or the other side of Calvin, both can use his words to
argue their case. Calvinists of the first type have been so
dominant that most Christians think of the Reformed
tradition as being without much interest in or even tolerance of religious experience. The second side of Calvin and
of the Reformed tradition has only recently been described.

A major source of the two very different interpretations
can be said to be rooted in the word "knowledge." Calvin
wrote repeatedly about the knowledge of God and of self.
He organized the *Institutes of the Christian Religion* around
the theme of the relationship between these two kinds of
knowledge. To know God is to know oneself and to know
oneself is to know God. These categories are central to his
theology. What has not been clear is how Calvin uses the
word "knowledge." Too often it has been interpreted as
intellectual, rational, and dispassionate, so that to know
God is to be able to describe God's qualities correctly, as
the Shorter Catechism does. Because Calvin is insistent
upon the inability of any human being really to know God,
he uses the word "know" in a much more existential way.
Bouwsma maintains that "experience" is a better word

than "know" to point to the way believers apprehend God's acts in the world. "Believers experience God as they experience—but can hardly be said to 'know'—thunder, one of Calvin's favorite metaphors for religious experience."[8] As thunder inspires us to awe, so the experience of God is so majestic and powerful as to defy expression. It does not lend itself to logical explanation.

Firsthand faith is the result of the experience of the holy within the life of the believer. It requires an internal and personal opening of the self to acceptance of and integration with the Divine. John Calvin declared that "as long as Christ remains outside us, we are separated from him, all that he has suffered and done for the salvation of the human race remains useless and of no value for us. Therefore, to share with us what he has received from the Father, he had to become ours and to dwell within us."[9]

The indwelling of Christ has been a favorite expression among many Reformed Christians to describe their experience of Christ's closeness. It may take many quite different forms. We are unique personalities and God respects that uniqueness. Religious experience that is central for one person may be completely alien for another. This does not mean that one is right and the other is wrong. In his work *Thoughts on the Revival of Religion in New England,* Jonathan Edwards sought to harmonize Calvinism with the profoundly powerful emotional forms of religious experience that accompanied the Great Awakening. Since the Calvinism that he had inherited was of the rigidly orthodox type, the effort was difficult and required a person of Edwards' brilliance. He found it necessary to distinguish among very different kinds of human experience and warned against those persons who "make their own experience the rule, and reject such and such things as are now professed and experienced, because they never felt them themselves."[10]

Human uniqueness and difference affect everything we do and have a profound impact on our interpretation and practice of religion. The Myers-Briggs Personality Inventory is an excellent tool for the discovery of one's own peculiarities and the acceptance of these as natural for the self. An introvert, for example, is much more comfortable with being alone and may be able easily to develop a style of prayer that is centered in silence, while an extrovert needs companionship and gets energy from being with others. Extroverts may have real difficulty with private prayer unless strengthened by commitments to others who share in the experiences, report to each other, and hold each other accountable.

Another example illustrates our response to experience and may have more to do with the two types of Calvinism than anything else. There are people who seek acceptance and approval from others and from themselves primarily on the basis of their performance and accomplishments. They want to excel and are usually quite competitive. Their emotions may be somewhat suspect because emotions cannot be controlled and may get out of hand. Such people are likely to have difficulty with religious experience because they do not want to surrender to their emotions. Their religious journey is apt to emphasize thought over experience. They are likely to be concerned about correct doctrine and the church as an institution. These people are dominated by what some have called their "left brain."

On the other hand, there are people whose primary orientation to life is through their feelings. They relate to other people best by being considerate and cooperative. They are concerned about how others feel and are eager to please them. Their religious life is more likely than that of our first group to be filled with sensations and dramatic experiences, and they may be impatient with anyone who suggests that they ought to hesitate and reflect before they act. They enjoy their experiences and may even come to equate the value of the experience with its intensity.

These two groups of people are often at odds with each other, each seeing the other as either sub-Christian or imbalanced. The intellectuals are worried about the dangers of mindless emotionalism, and the feeling people are worried about intellectual dryness and sterility. Serious divisions have taken place in the church over these two

approaches to the Christian life. Among American Presbyterians and Congregationalists, the Old Side/New Side or
Old Light/New Light division in the early eighteenth century was rooted in just this conflict, between those who
stressed theological correctness and those who supported
the Great Awakening and the appeal to the emotions so
closely connected with it.

A great danger that we all face in our pilgrimage to come
to terms with God's particular calling for us is that we may
mistake the way that seems right for us as the only way,
which must be followed by everyone. An even greater
danger is that we may attempt to force ourselves to have the
experiences of other people whom we trust and value,
because it seems that unless we have experiences that
resemble theirs we are not real Christians. That is the real
threat of the cults—they demand that everyone have the
same religious experience and speak about that experience
in the same words and images. Human uniqueness is
denied in the name of uniformity, and people are required
to conform or leave. Much energy goes into the effort to
have the expected religious experiences. Terrible pain accompanies the failure to achieve the sought-after goal.
People blame themselves for not being able to conform,
or they may become angry at God and embittered and
alienated from Christian faith itself. After an extensive
discussion of the various ways in which one may become
open to God, Frank Laubach insists, "Any method, absolutely any method is *your* method if you find it opens the
doors toward heaven and helps you gain close contact with
God. And it is not *your* method, no matter who does it, if
it does not succeed in doing that."[11] To follow Laubach's
advice is to avoid a great deal of painful effort in self-
deception, through which we attempt to be something that
we are not.

If we can acknowledge that there is more to the world
than our senses can identify, we are at least open to
spiritual experience as a possibility. If we can escape from
our need to screen out or repress our own experiences when
they do not fit our rational explanations of the way the

universe operates, we may be startled into new awareness of God's nearness. We must put aside our sense of shame when our own experiences are different from those around us. Then we may come to respect God's way of treating us through our uniqueness. It is the constant and exhausting struggle to conform that prevents many people from honestly acknowledging their own religious experiences.

In spite of hesitation and fear, people in our time continue to have experiences that defy explanation. They may be uncomfortable with them, they may not want to speak about them to others, but they will admit to having them when they are convinced that they will not be dismissed or scorned for speaking about them. If we really believe that God is love, then it follows that God is always seeking relationship. Love cannot remain aloof and removed from the one who is loved. The lover is driven by love to express love to the beloved. Christian faith declares that love is the essence of God; thus we cannot escape the conclusion that God is continually seeking relationship with human beings. We may not acknowledge that divine seeking. We may dismiss our own experiences as odd coincidences or mental confusion. We may even wonder about temporary insanity, but we have experiences that draw us beyond the everyday world of ordinary sense experience into the realms of the unexplainable.

Because God is the Divine Lover who is constantly seeking communion with us, we can discover many different ways that God touches us. The ways vary with our temperament and life situation. Some of us are more open to certain kinds of experience. However we experience God, the moment of encounter is one that can change our life.

1. Conversion experiences: People are changed, sometimes quickly, by an experience of radical reorientation of their lives. It may come about by an act of faith which replaces unfaith or by a more passive and gradually developing sense of God's grace as real for them. It may be the result of shedding a narrow, inherited faith and discovering a faith that is appropriate for the mature adult person. Conversion does not always mean that one goes from unbelief to belief; it may be the experience of moving from secondhand to firsthand faith. However conversion comes about, it is certainly a form of spiritual experience, and all those people who have had such experiences can give testimony to the power they discovered. Howard Thurman describes the experience of conversion as a crisis in which the individual is able to experience the grace of God in spite of a sense of personal unworthiness. In this situation the individual is able to accept a new way of life as a gift from the dramatic action of God's Spirit. "For many this is the encounter with the living Christ, and in His name or in His Spirit they go forth into newness of life."[12]

Protestant Christianity has cherished the conversion experience to the point that, at times, it has insisted on evidence of conversion for admission into the church. There is a deep and strong sense of the reality of the Divine in those people whose conversion experience is still real for them. The Puritans were vividly aware of the importance of conversion in the life of the believer, but conversion was the opening to a new and deeper form of spirituality and not complete by itself.[13] Reformed Protestants have generally insisted that the Christian life is one of gradual growth in the grace of sanctification toward union with Christ, and that conversion is a very important initial event in that pilgrimage, but only a beginning.

One of the problems with conversion experiences is that they may replace the ongoing recognition of God's continuing work in our lives. Conversion can be seen as an end in itself instead of the beginning of a process of growth. Thus Thurman warns, "These energies must be geared to the specific demands of the new life."[14] Unless such a forward direction of the spontaneous energy of the conversion experience takes place, people can get stuck, endlessly repeating the same story over and over and failing to grow in faith.

2. Ecstatic experiences: There is historical evidence that there are times in the life of the church when particular dramatic experiences of spiritual healing, prophecy, and speaking in tongues are more common than at other times. People who have such experiences have an intensity to their faith that is sometimes missing in the lives of those who have not had such experiences. God, through the power of the Holy Spirit, has entered their lives, and the particular experience is seen as evidence of that divine touch. Morton Kelsey is one of the few scholars who have explored charismatic experiences with sensitivity and compassion, as can be seen in several of his books, including *Transcend* and *Discernment.*

Spiritual pride is a danger that may spoil the beauty of the ecstatic experience whenever people come to believe that they are closer to God or more deserving of such an experience than those who have not been so touched. Jonathan Edwards warned that when people talk a great deal about religion, it may be from either a good or a bad cause. "A person may be overfull of talk of his own experiences; commonly falling upon it, everywhere, and in all companies; and when it is so, it is rather a dark sign than a good one."[15] We tend to react negatively to people who insist on speaking too much of their own religious experience. They begin to sound hollow and insincere.

It also needs to be said that those who seem to put too much emphasis on their charismatic experience may be reacting to the demeaning of their experience by others. It frequently happens that when some people have such direct experiences of the Holy Spirit they are objects of fear, mistrust, and rejection by other church members. This makes them place even more emphasis on their experience as a means of protecting themselves from attack. The gap between so-called "charismatics" and the rest of a congregation may widen into a split, which is then used to justify the conviction that it is the charismatic experience itself which is the cause of the division.

Because Reformed Christians have had difficulty integrating their emotions with their faith, the fear of the charismatic experience has been particularly evident. Yet because we have not satisfied our emotional needs, we are particularly vulnerable to such experiences as a breakthrough into emotional depth.

3. Visionary and auditory experiences: Although somewhat more rare than the first two examples, there are many people who have heard voices or seen visions which they believe have not come from their own imaginations but are visitations from God. Acting on the voice or following the vision may be important for such a person as a step of obedience and the results may turn out to be significant for the individual and for people around the person.

Most often these visions and voices come to people through their dreams. In our dreams we are less likely to be blocked from receptivity and are more vulnerable to experiences we might otherwise dismiss or fail to recognize. Although he possessed no method for interpreting dreams and did not attempt to do so, Calvin recognized their importance: "Why is it that the soul not only vaguely roves about but conceives many useful things, ponders concerning many, even divines the future—all while man sleeps? What ought we to say here except that the signs of immortality which have been implanted in man cannot be effaced?"[16]

The danger with any visionary or auditory experience is that people can easily mistake their own deeply held desires for visitations from God and may manufacture the experiences without being aware of it. Some forms of mental illness affect people by erasing the boundary between reality and fantasy, so that they are convinced that they are hearing voices or seeing visions. It is very difficult to distinguish between genuine visitations of God and hallucinations. Edwards warns, "The devil can counterfeit all the saving operations and graces of the Spirit of God, so he can counterfeit . . . those effects of God's Spirit which are special, divine, and sanctifying."[17] The dangers of pride and self-deception, though great, do not invalidate the experiences of healthy people, who are frequently led by their experiences to make sacrifices on behalf of others in beautiful ways.

4. Intuitive experiences: These are very common moments in which one has an inner sense of what is needed in a particular situation, or in which insight provides a clue as to what is *really* going on in the midst of what may otherwise appear only confusion. Most people have had experiences of deep personal indecision, wondering what to do in a particular situation and uncertain of what should be the solution. The confusion may have defied all attempts at resolution. Thinking through all the possibilities provided no clarity and may have only intensified the confusion. Then, suddenly, one morning all became clear, and the answer was obvious. The answer seemed to have been provided by another, and an inner peace was also present, with no second thoughts.

A similar human experience is that of congruence or, as we generally call it, "coincidence." One event in life fits completely with another in such a way that we know that we did nothing to make these events come together. It may be, for example, that we wake up one morning thinking about some friend we have not seen for a long time. We puzzle about this, and only later discover that the individual we had remembered was in great trouble at the very moment we were thinking of this person. In a more positive vein, we may receive a letter or phone call the morning after dreaming about some friend from long ago.

These experiences defy explanation. Calvin recognized the variety of human experiences of unexplained mystery: "Manifold indeed is the nimbleness of the soul with which it surveys heaven and earth, joins past to future, retains in memory something heard long before, nay, pictures to itself whatever it pleases. Manifold also is the skill with which it devises things incredible, and which is the mother of so many marvelous devices. These are unfailingly signs of divinity in man."[18]

As with all other experiences of mystery, there is some danger of mistaking self-will for God's presence. There are people who are completely convinced that they have received messages from God even when these "messages" lead them to acts that go against reason and morality.

5. Transcendent experiences: There are times when we are caught off guard by an experience in which we forget ourselves at least momentarily and are captured by the wonder of life. In the presence of a glorious sunset or the magic of a rainbow, for example, we are spellbound and sense that we are not alone in an alien universe. A great piece of music may have a similar effect on us. For others of us, the experience of being drawn out of ourselves may occur in times of great stress or of great relief from stress. In time of great personal loss—whether the loss of a loved one, the loss of a job, or the loss of health—we may discover that life takes on more rather than less meaning. Painful though the experience may be, it has the effect of prodding us into depths we had not previously imagined possible.

It is also common for people to discover new meaning as a result of a close call, when they have come near to death. Those who have been in serious accidents frequently testify that they began to wonder, in a new way, about the gift of life and its meaning. When our usual barriers are down and we are not in full control of our situation, we are most open to and receptive of the mystery and the presence of God. We are most likely, also, to know that we need to be alone and to come to terms with the meaning of life for ourselves.

6. Incarnational experiences: The experience of the divine may be made known through other people who show love so well that they represent the love of God for us. Having another person love us when we know only too well our own unlovableness, or being forgiven by another for something hurtful we have done, may serve as a pointer to the divine and cause us to reclaim a faith that has grown dim.

The experience of the birth of a baby is another such incarnational experience, in which the wonder and mystery of a new life cause us to marvel at God as the source of life in a more deeply personal way. Calvin was convinced that human reproduction was a revelatory sign of God's faithfulness. "If ingratitude did not put upon our eyes the veil of stupidity, we would be ravished with admiration at every childbirth in the world."[19]

Sexuality can be another way in which the experience of God can be mediated through another person. There is a connection between spirituality and sexuality although, because of the mind-body split that plagues Christians, we have trouble acknowledging this reality. Our own experience, however, reveals to us that sex and spirit are related. When we are sexually involved in a committed relationship with another person, we discover a central metaphor of our relationship with God, for sexuality is an expression of our need for reunion and wholeness that may be satisfied only in intimacy with another. We are not disembodied spirits, and our physical encounters with other persons will, if we let them, speak to us of that which is beyond the moment.

This is only a partial list of the different kinds of religious experience. People speak about the presence of God when they are with someone at the time of death. Still others are encountered by God when they are forced to spend a period of time alone. All people have experiences of God of some kind, because there is more to life than we usually recognize. We may not remember these special moments; we may try to explain them away; we may even be frightened by them—but as we reflect upon life, we cannot dismiss the reality of our experience of God with rational explanations alone.

In spite of the wide differences among people and their experience of God, it is possible to discern some common characteristics of spiritual experiences that are healthy and in harmony with the broad sweep of Christian tradition. These characteristics help us to measure our own experience and determine whether or not it is genuine. Those experiences which are not in harmony with these characteristics should be properly suspect; they may be deceptive, dangerous, or destructive.

1. The experience of the holy is ordinarily something that people do not seek out. It is much more likely to be something that occurs to them while they are going about some other activity. This is certainly true in the biblical stories of encounters with God. For Saul, the encounter with the risen Christ took place while he was trying to get rid of Christians. For Moses it took place while he was going about his work of caring for his father-in-law's flock. There are, of course, activities that can make us more vulnerable and open to encounters with God, but we need to be careful about efforts to *create* such experiences for ourselves.

The Reformed tradition has always been deeply concerned about the dangers of idolatry. Efforts to achieve special experiences for ourselves easily fall into the trap of being idolatrous. People can get caught up in the desperate need to imagine a god of their own and strive to make themselves have sensations that will reinforce their images. People who are overeager to seek out the unusual may miss the God of the ordinary.

2. The experience of God has the element of awe. In the scriptural record, those who have been encountered by God nearly always have to be reassured by such expressions as "Fear not." They are terrified by what has happened to them. They meet the holy God, and they are conscious of the distance between themselves and God. Moses must put off his sandals, Jacob is wounded in the thigh, Isaiah is aware of the uncleanness of his lips, and Saul is blinded.

Whenever people claim to have experiences of God that are described only in terms of being lovely and wonderful and feeling good, we must ask about what God they have encountered. Calvin goes so far as to say, "Whenever the feeblest ray of the Divine glory bursts upon us, we cannot avoid being alarmed."[20] Without some sense of awe, the experience of God is reduced to manufacturing a convenient idol who can be easily met on our own level and treated like a pal. God's powerful love is never a comfortable private possession and will always include both a sense of inner peace and an uncomfortable experience of awe.

3. The experience of God always demands something of a person, and often that demand requires the person to accomplish something difficult. A reluctant Moses is sent to lead God's people out of slavery. Isaiah is called to proclaim a message which he knows will cause him personal pain. Saul is required to become the apostle of the very faith that he has sworn to oppose and destroy. People are required to take up tasks, to make changes, or to let go of something precious.

Any asserted experience of God that demands nothing and only confirms the person's present life is certainly very different from biblical experiences. Emily Herman describes the aftereffects of what she calls "baptismal moments." They are "always followed by a temptation in the wilderness; the unveiling of beauty always involves a stern ethical choice. Upon the seer rests the special obligation to be obedient to the heavenly vision, and obedience is not a natural instinct; it is a matter of long training, of continuous moral discipline."[21] God's love reaches out to us, but not just for our sakes alone. It is a love that would shape us as instruments of God's wider concern for other people. The key to right understanding of all spiritual experience is in our obedience. Any other standard of evaluation of religious experience can be distorted or used for selfish purposes. Calvin declared, "Not only faith, perfect and in every way complete, but all right knowledge of God is born of obedience."[22]

4. Confirmation of the spiritual experience should be sought from others we trust. All of us need to have other people in our lives to whom we can turn for guidance and discernment about our own experiences. Because we so easily misread and misinterpret our experiences, self-discernment can be very dangerous. Many people have failed to distinguish between psychosis and what they have believed to be visitations by God. They have done damage to themselves and to others by following the leading as they have sensed it. When trusted friends tell us to be careful, we need to pay attention. All of us need to have friendships in

which we trust each other enough that we have the courage to share our experiences with the other. We need friends whom we can trust with sufficient confidence that we can tell them what has happened to us without fear of ridicule. At the same time, we need to trust their wisdom enough to accept that it may lead them to a cautiously healthy suspicion of our own interpretation of our experience.

These four guidelines are important for all people, because there is always the temptation to use religious experience as a way to get something for ourselves and to gain new control over our lives. There are many self-proclaimed religious leaders who promise just such results from doing as they say. They promise that if the hearer will only follow instructions (usually sending in money), blessings will surely follow and one's life will go well. They promise that health, success, wealth, and popularity are the results of right belief. This promise is very appealing, because it meets us in the midst of our universal human struggle. No one of us has life quite the way he or she wants it. We would all like to have things a little easier, for the pieces to fall into place a bit more neatly. At least once in a while we all wonder "what if" about ourselves. What if I had a better physique or were wittier or had more education? We look around at other people and they seem to have what we lack, and we become envious of them. That makes us all easy prey for the promises that offer a life without struggle or pain.

Perhaps the greatest illusion in seeking only what we want from God is that we are trying to keep control over our lives when we really know at a deep level that control is the one element we cannot have. Control is a goal that always disappoints us. Part of being human is to know that our lives are not in our own power. We cannot determine the day of our death, we cannot decide who will love us, and we cannot finally determine with any certainty our physical or mental condition. Some of what we want for ourselves will not happen, and this lack does not mean that God has abandoned us. We do not need a new technique so much as we need a new motive for the development of our spirituality. The exhausting effort to try to maintain the pretense of control is one that drives us to seek God as the rescuer. We bargain with God and promise to do something sacrificial if only God will grant our request. Most of the time such efforts to use God do not work out.

If the motive behind our spiritual quest is an increase of control over our lives, we run several risks. What if life does not work out as some religious leaders have promised? How will we feel when we are let down by unfulfilled expectations? Many bitterly disappointed people once believed that by performing the correct spiritual activities they could get something important for themselves, but have not achieved the desired result. They have become cynical and disillusioned by the experience, and may even think that God has rejected them or let them down.

Superstition tries to *use* the power of God to achieve personal goals. All of us really know that this is not possible. God is not simply one of us on a grander scale. The very freedom of God is the source of our hope, for such a God is free to love us when we are most unlovable.

In his book *Will and Spirit,* Gerald May says that we must finally come to the realization that our efforts to control God must be abandoned. "Slowly, if one is willing to accept some humility, the situation becomes clear. It is not for us to use the power of mystery, but for us to be used by it. We do not embrace it in our arms, it embraces us. We do not capture it but are captured by it."[23] When we come to this realization, we can either become cynical and try to make the most of life on our own, or we can decide that there is a power that makes a difference in our lives. God is the One who gives life and God is the ultimate provider.

It is no accident that the people most likely to be eager for a personal experience of God in their lives are those who have been forced to discover, often at considerable pain, that they are not in control. Such people have been through tragedy, their lives have been torn apart by divorce, failure, death of a loved one, sexual confusion, disease, or the inability to meet the expectations of others. They discover to their deep disappointment that the high-sounding schemes that seem to work for other people do not work for them, and they have been forced to come to terms with this fact.

In March of 1978 the United Presbyterian Church did a study on the devotional habits of its people, called "Prayer, Religious Practices, and Sources for Christian Growth." Church members, officers, and ministers were asked how often they prayed and read the Bible and how much these practices meant to them. The discovery was that the less control people had over their lives the more likely they were to be deeply involved in seeking a personal relationship with God. Women were more likely than men to pray and to view prayer as very important for their lives, younger and older people more likely than people in their middle years, poor people more likely than rich people, and divorced or widowed people more likely than married people.[24] When we are without the defenses of being able to pretend that we are in charge, we are more willing to let go. We are more eager for a personal relationship with the God who may upset our plans and disrupt our conveniences. We are more open to experiences of God.

The illusion of control is hard to break. We give it up only after a great struggle, because deeply ingrained in us is our desire to run things our way. The experience of those who have suffered the painful collapse of their carefully constructed world is that they have a new openness to God. Hurting people are more likely to see God as merciful and loving than are people who seem to live without great suffering. The more deeply people are wounded by the experience of life, the more they have a desperate need for God's love. It *hurts* deeply to experience the breaking apart of dreams and the shattering of hopes and plans, but it *heals* powerfully to discover in our own experience that in the midst of the pain and brokenness, God becomes real and present for us.

Because God is the Divine Lover who seeks us out, God will use different methods to reach us. For some, the door appears to be opened by a divine entrance against the person's will. For most, the discovery of God's reality comes much more gently or gradually. For still others, and we shall never know why, the discovery never takes place at all. These people continue to live out their lives, things continue to work out reasonably well for them, and they can believe that they are in such control that they really do not need God very much.

Most of us are blessed by experiences in which the love of God is made real for us. Our problem is that we are not paying attention, and therefore miss the blessing of discovering the intimate presence of God in our everyday lives. To be aware, awake, and attentive is to discover the love that will not let us go, the love that is the ground of all our strength and hope.

> Command me what thou wilt, O Lord, give me but strength to obey thee, be thy terms ever so severe. O let us never part. I resign my will, my liberty, my choice, to thee: I stand divested of the world, and ask only thy love as my inheritance. Give or deny me what thou wilt, I leave all the circumstances of my future time in thy hands: let the Lord guide me continually: here I am, do with me what seemeth good in thy sight: only do not say, Thou hast no pleasure in me. Let me not live to dishonour thee, to bring a reproach on thy name, to profane the blood of the Son of God, and grieve the Spirit of grace. O take not thy loving kindness from me, nor suffer thy faithfulness to fail. Thou hast sworn by thy holiness, and thou wilt not lie to the seed of thy servants; thou hast sworn, that the generation of the righteous shall be blessed; vest me with this character, O my God, and fulfill this promise to a worthless creature.
>
> Elizabeth Rowe[25]

NOTES

1. Presbyterian Church (U.S.A.), *The Book of Confessions* (New York and Atlanta: Office of the General Assembly, 1983), 3.12.

2. Augustine, *The Confessions of Saint Augustine,* trans. Edward B. Pusey (New York: Random House, Modern Library, 1949), p. 3.

3. John Calvin, *Institutes of the Christian Religion,* ed. John T. McNeill, trans. Ford Lewis Battles (Philadelphia: Westminster Press, 1960), I, III, 1, p. 45.

4. Morton Kelsey, *Transcend: A Guide to the Spiritual Quest* (New York: Crossroad, 1981), p. 23.

5. William Bouwsma, *John Calvin: A Sixteenth-Century Portrait* (New York: Oxford University Press, 1987), p. 230.

6. *Book of Confessions,* 7.0004.

7. Bouwsma, *John Calvin,* p. 231.

8. Bouswma, William, "The Spirituality of John Calvin," in *Christian Spirituality: High Middle Ages and Reformation,* vol. 17, *World Spirituality: An Encyclopedic History of the Religious Quest,* ed. Jill Raitt, Bernard McGinn, and John Meyendorff (New York: Crossroad, 1987), p. 323.

9. Calvin, *Institutes,* III, I, 1, p. 537.

10. Jonathan Edwards, "Thoughts on the Revival of Religion in New England, 1742," in *Edwards on Revivals* (New York: Dunning & Spaulding, 1832), p. 139.

11. Frank Laubach, *Channels of Spiritual Power* (Westwood, N.J.: Fleming H. Revell, 1954), p. 95.

12. Howard Thurman, *Disciplines of the Spirit* (New York: Harper & Row, 1963), p. 23.

13. Charles Hambrick-Stowe, *The Practice of Piety: Puritan Devotional Disciplines in Seventeenth-Century New England* (Chapel Hill, N.C.: University of North Carolina Press, 1982), p. 89.

14. Thurman, *Disciplines of the Spirit,* p. 25.

15. Jonathan Edwards, *Religious Affections,* ed. John E. Smith (New Haven, Conn.: Yale University Press, 1959), p. 137.

16. Calvin, *Institutes,* I, V, 5, p. 57.

17. Edwards, *Religious Affections,* p. 158.

18. Calvin, *Institutes,* I, V, 5, p. 57.

19. John Calvin, *Commentaries: The Book of Psalms,* trans. James Anderson (Grand Rapids: Baker Book House, 1984), 22:10, vol. 1, p. 369.

20. John Calvin, *Commentary on a Harmony of the Evangelists,* trans. William Pringle (Grand Rapids: Wm. B. Eerdmans Publishing Co., 1949), Luke 1:20, vol. 1, p. 34.

21. Emily Herman, *The Meaning and Value of Mysticism* (New York: George H. Doran, 1925), p. 137.

22. Calvin, *Institutes,* I, VI, 2, p. 72.

23. Gerald May, *Will and Spirit* (San Francisco: Harper & Row, 1982), p. 35.

24. "Prayer, Religious Practices, and Sources for Christian Growth," *Presbyterian Panel,* March 1978, p. 9.

25. Elizabeth Rowe, *Devout Exercises of the Heart,* ed. Isaac Watts (Baltimore: J. Kingston, 1811), p. 199.

2

Reformed Spirituality: Problems and Possibilities

Q. What is true faith?
A. It is not only a certain knowledge by which I accept as true all that God has revealed to us in his Word, but also a wholehearted trust which the Holy Spirit creates in me through the gospel, that, not only to others, but to me also God has given the forgiveness of sins, everlasting righteousness and salvation, out of sheer grace solely for the sake of Christ's saving work.

The Heidelberg Catechism[1]

The word "spirituality" makes many Reformed Protestants uncomfortable. It suggests a realm of life opposed to and distinct from material life. Those who use the word often believe in the division of life into two separate and independent or even competing arenas. An unfair caricature of spirituality, this separation is based on the observation of Christians who think themselves spiritual and believe that they are above the ordinary struggles, confusions, and follies of the rest of humanity. There are just enough such people in the church to sustain misconceptions of spirituality.

Spirituality is the pattern by which we shape our lives in response to our experience of God as a very real presence in and around us. Gordon Wakefield defines "spiritual" by saying that it is used "to describe those attitudes, beliefs, practices which animate people's lives and help them to reach toward super-sensible realities."[2] To be spiritual is to take seriously our consciousness of God's presence and to live in such a way that the presence of God is central in all that we do. This awareness of God is not automatic, nor can it be brought about by any particular technique. We can, however, open ourselves to the already present God by deliberately cultivating certain disciplines of mind and will.

Within the Reformed tradition, the word that has been used most commonly to mean spirituality is "piety." Most contemporary Protestants react negatively to the word "piety" or to anything that remotely reminds them of that word. Piety sounds narrowly judgmental and self-righteous. It often has the overtones of a form of religion that is afraid of finding any joy in the created order, opting instead for a stern and grim, dutiful determination to keep rigid rules. But piety is nothing more than the pattern by which we shape our lives before God in grateful obedience to what God has done for us. Calvin's definition of piety is helpful in understanding its scope: "I call 'piety' that reverence joined with love of God which the knowledge of [God's] benefits induces."[3] All of us, in this sense, have a piety. All of us acknowledge to some degree that there are responsible ways of being Christian, that there are *some* responsibilities that are inherent in our faith and other actions that we must reject in our lives. Our piety is the way we exercise our Christian freedom as people whose lives have been touched by grace and who are thus keenly aware of being responsible to God. Our piety is the way we live our lives responding to God's presence by attending carefully to that presence.

Christian piety is not the unique possession of a certain "pious" group. It is the way all Christians exercise responsible freedom before God in the world. Because piety takes many forms, we may not identify another person's Christian practice by that name. There are forms of piety that emphasize the mind and are reflective, and other forms that emphasize the emotions and are passionate. There are pieties that are action-oriented and take place in groups, and others that are more passive and solitary. In spite of stereotypes we have of both "spirituality" and "piety," one cannot be a Christian without them.

Because of suspicion about spirituality within the Reformed tradition, frequently when persons have felt the proddings of the Spirit in their own lives they have either kept quiet about the experience or have moved to another tradition in order to be comfortable to speak about what has happened to them. Yet Reformed Christians are not different from other Christians. The survey of Presbyterians in March 1978 titled "Prayer, Religious Practices, and Sources for Christian Growth" asked this question: "Would you say that you have had a religious or mystical experience(s), i.e., a moment of sudden religious insight or awakening?" Nearly half of the church members responded by agreeing with "To a great extent" as their reply. Only 36 percent of the members answered "No."[4] There is an unarticulated and often unrecognized experiential form of spirituality among persons in the Reformed tradition.

The chief purpose of all people is "to glorify God, and to enjoy [God] forever."[5] The Westminster Shorter Catechism provides a good way to describe the practice of Reformed spirituality. It includes two elements that are a healthy corrective to distorted ideas of what it means to be spiritual. First, we glorify God and not ourselves. The true purpose of Christian spirituality is not what we do for ourselves or how holy we may appear to others. It is how we point beyond ourselves and bear witness to the majesty and love of God. A God-centered spirituality brings glory to God rather than credit to ourselves. We glorify God both in our inward relationship to God and in living out faith in our daily lives. We bring glory to God or we dishonor God by our betrayal of what we are called to be and do.

We are also, according to this Catechism, "to enjoy [God]." Piety or spirituality is not a dreary negation of everything in the world; the challenge of Reformed piety is to discover the joy of obedient discipleship. John Calvin insisted that when we are free from the law and its harsh requirements, we "will cheerfully and with great eagerness answer and follow [God's] leading."[6] We grant, however, that all too frequently piety has been an expression of self-righteous negativity and grim determination. Emily Herman observed this distorted form of piety and attributed to it Christians' frequent reluctance to begin the inward journey. "They recall a time when even the hearts of little children were shadowed over by a stern and legal conception of God, and when saints, delivered from a miry pit and set upon a rock, went their way with a new sigh rather than a new song in their mouth."[7]

Most contemporary American Protestants would agree that too much legalistic severity is dangerous—for example, in defining the Christian life as enjoying nothing and rejecting all the good gifts of the Creator. We may also need to be reminded of the risk of too much leniency, which, in the name of Christian freedom, indulges every selfish whim, draws no boundaries, and never says no to anything. The Reformed tradition has, at its best, taught that we are to give thanks for the created order, and has therefore been able to rejoice in the gifts of earthly living. The appropriate enjoyment of life and its pleasures is part of Reformed piety, despite an image of Calvin and his successors as a dour and cheerless lot.

Reformed Resistances

Any attempt to develop a spirituality that is rooted in and appropriate to the situation and needs of Reformed Protestants must come to terms with the deeply ingrained suspicion toward the words "spirituality" and "piety" and an equally strong resistance toward the practices these words represent.

Class Bias

One of the sources of this resistance is found in the social class of Reformed Protestants. Our resistance toward spiritual language and practice has much to do with our position in society. As middle-class people, we value control, cherish the intellect, fear our emotions, and emphasize what can be *done*. We also tend to be relatively well off and therefore somewhat satisfied with our lives. All these tendencies make traditional practices of spirituality alien to our basic mentality. Spirituality demands letting go of control, taking the emotions seriously, and emphasizing *being* as of equal value with doing. Middle-class people are busy people and are afraid of empty time and idleness. Time for prayer or meditation may seem like frivolously wasted time. So, too, middle-class people, especially men, have valued the mind and its ability to exercise control and to bring order to situations, and have been suspicious of their own feelings.

Protestants who have experienced oppression and who have not been as securely middle class are much more receptive to the workings of the Spirit. African Americans certainly demonstrate this. They are not afraid of feelings, not so deeply committed to results, and have not experienced control as an idol to which they need to cling. Their spirituality has a freedom about it that is often looked upon wistfully by white Protestants but which cannot be easily appropriated without imitating and thus demeaning or mocking it.

Growing out of the negativity of our class bias are some prejudices rooted in historical experience that have produced particular emphases and suspicions within the Reformed tradition. These have furthered the resistance toward practices that are usually identified with the Christian spiritual tradition.

Rejection of Works

Because the Reformers insisted on the centrality of grace as God's freely given gift, any spiritual practice that could suggest that grace could be earned or deserved came under their utter and total condemnation. Calvin insisted on the centrality of grace for salvation. He wished to make it very clear that "our righteousness is not in us but in Christ, that we possess it only because we are partakers in Christ; indeed, with him we possess all its riches."[8] The passage from the Heidelberg Catechism with which this chapter begins strongly declares this message. The Holy Spirit is the source of the faith within us. No spiritual act that we do can come from our natural powers; it must be from the inspiration of the Holy Spirit which resurrects our dead souls, opens our blind eyes, and enables us to have the strength to obey God. Without this divinely given inspiration we remain stubbornly closed to God.

These early Protestants were convinced that many medieval spiritual practices were human efforts to bridge the gap that sin had created and to do so from the human side. Therefore, they rejected many long-established methods of spiritual formation that had provided guidance for people throughout the centuries. It is true that certain spiritual practices used images such as that of a "ladder" to God and, whether intended or not, often gave the impression that one could work one's way from a nonspiritual condition to a state of union with God by following a particular disciplined method. The discipline varied with the particular tradition, but generally entailed a series of practices or steps that were quite well defined and required one's whole attention. It thus worked best in monastic settings in which people were freed from other responsibilities and enabled to devote their whole time to the pursuit of the spiritual life.

In spite of their rejection of what they labeled "works righteousness," the Reformers were not hostile to all the medieval disciplines of the spiritual life. Consistently, they held in high regard the necessity of private or secret prayer, family meditation, and devotional reflection on the scriptures. Many medieval devotional practices were strongly commended to Reformed Protestants by their pastors and are described in the devotional manuals they produced. These private exercises of the devotional life were always to be held in balance with the public means of grace: preaching, singing, corporate prayer and study, and a carefully prepared-for observance of the sacraments. The Scottish pastor and political activist Samuel Rutherford, in a letter of advice to John Gordon, strongly suggests the use of forms as he advises, "Strive to make prayer, and reading, and holy company, and holy conference your delight; and when delight cometh in, ye shall by little and little smell the sweetness of Christ."[9] Although grace is given by God without our deserving, we open ourselves to be receivers of that grace when we place ourselves at God's disposal. The "means of grace" are those practices by which the believer becomes receptive to God, attentive to what God may be demanding, and responsive to the leading of the Holy Spirit.

One of the most popular Protestant religious paintings, frequently used in stained-glass windows, portrays Christ standing at the door and knocking. It is important to note that the door has no handle. It can only be opened from inside. Christ does not force himself upon the soul but gently knocks, awaiting admission from within. The traditional practices of Christian spirituality are ways of attending to the knocking and of unbolting the locks from within, so as to be open to the possibility of having that door ready to be opened to the living Christ.

In our zeal as Reformed Protestants to avoid any semblance of salvation by human works, we need to accept the fact that we have become overly negative about practices that were never intended to earn merit. The great medieval mystics did not claim that one could earn salvation by following their particular way. They insisted that any suggested practice or discipline was a response to God's graciousness, an act of thanksgiving, and an answer to God's invitation to enter into a deeper relationship.

Rejection of Individualism

The Reformed tradition has been deeply suspicious of privatized religion in any form. Thus, any piety that appears to be content with a personal relationship with Jesus, and which shuns or belittles the horizontal dimension of discipleship, is suspect. Any spiritual practice that produces a withdrawal of concern for what is going on in the world and loss of concern for other people has been rejected by Reformed piety as contrary to Christ's spirit.

Calvin was insistent upon the necessity for all Christians to seek guidance and counsel for others and condemned private forms of piety. He ridiculed those who "are led either by pride, dislike, or rivalry to the conviction that they can profit enough from private reading and meditation; hence they despise public assemblies and deem preaching superfluous."[10] He was attacking what he believed to be the weakness of some Anabaptist teachings and practice. There are still such people today, who believe that the church comes between them and their experiences of the Divine and gets in the way of their spiritual development. They have, thus, given up on the church.

One of the chief characteristics of the Reformed tradition is an emphasis on God's redemption of a people. God calls a community into being in order for it to participate in God's saving work in the context of a covenant. This insistence upon the corporate nature of the Christian life has not always been very receptive to private experiences of God's presence, particularly if these experiences lead people to disdain the community of faith or to feel that they are, in some way, superior to their brothers and sisters in the faith. In fact, nearly every responsible writer in the field of spirituality stresses the obligation to use the closeness with God that may be found as a source of strength for service to others. The distinction between private and public spirituality is a destructive caricature of Christian spirituality. The principal source for personal spiritual depth may be private or corporate disciplines, or a combination of both.

One of the reasons for the negative attitude toward private religious practice springs from a deeply held Reformed conviction that it is not possible to have pure motives. Reformed Christians take seriously the pervasiveness of sin. Individuals regularly need the corrective of the whole community of faith, lest their religious experience be distorted and they move into realms of fantasy, mistaking their own desires for the leading of the Holy Spirit. At the very heart of the Reformed understanding of the Christian life is the insistence that it be corporate.

Any authentic Reformed piety will need to take the whole community of faith very seriously. It will be a spiritual life which subjects itself to others for advice. In common worship people will seek correction. That is why corporate worship, hearing the Word preached, and sharing in the common administration of the Sacraments are so central for any Reformed understanding of the spiritual life. We are redeemed as a community, and not merely as lone individuals. We learn the meaning of the faith as we share together in worship. We are continually being reminded of who we are by our common exposure to the Word of God as it is heard with understanding. We learn to pray by sharing in the life of prayer of the whole church gathered. Calvin's appreciation for the necessity of the gathered community is clear when he declares that we partake of salvation when we are "gathered together into one body, under the same Head" and that the most significant value in this gathering is that we "have mutual care one of another" so that we are not so engrossed in our own advantage or interest and are not "indifferent to the welfare and happiness of others."[11] We gather not just to receive from the community, but also to give of our strength, faith, and encouragement.

While we should treasure the necessity for the communal nature of all spirituality, it needs to be said that we have often been so suspicious of private religious experiences and practices that they have been devalued. As we stated earlier, there is a subtle pressure to keep any very deep personal experiences to oneself or even to deny having them. The inner life has been neglected to the point that many Reformed Christians are obedient and faithful out of a sense of loyalty and duty, but without much joy and enthusiasm.

There has been, nevertheless, a historical place for the practice of private spiritual discipline within the Reformed tradition, although it has been forgotten by many people. Calvin defined prayer as something "secret," pointing out that Jesus withdrew to a quiet spot for prayer. Thus Calvin says that prayer is "principally lodged in the heart and requires a tranquillity far from all our teeming cares."[12] The necessity for private prayer is also stressed by the Reformed writer Matthew Henry. In his influential classic on devotional practice, *A Method of Prayer,* he deals with three different settings for prayer: public, family, and secret, or private. They belong together, and each has a way of reinforcing and strengthening the others.

From the time of the Westminster Assembly in the 1640s until very recently, the Westminster Directory for the Worship of God contained a listing of the four parts of secret or private worship: prayer, reading scripture, holy meditation, and serious self-examination. In the newest edition of the Directory for Worship, these are expanded to include: reading scripture, prayer, silent waiting upon God, meditation upon the Word, self-offering, and commitments to service.[13] Each of these parts of secret worship is balanced by public worship and kept honest when shared with others, but they must be done alone if they are to have meaning. Christians who do not pray in private have very little to bring to public prayer. Christians who never read their Bibles by themselves have little understanding or love for scripture to enable them to be prepared to hear it preached. Calvin summed up this dual need for private and public prayer: "Whoever refused to pray in the holy assembly of the godly knows not what it is to pray individually, or in a secret spot, or at home." Likewise he writes that those who neglect "to pray alone and in private, however unremittingly" they may "frequent public assemblies," there contrive only "windy prayers," for they really defer to human opinion rather than to the "secret judgment of God."[14]

The balance between private and public forms of piety in the spiritual life is always a difficult one to maintain. Our fear of the dangers of too much emphasis on the private has produced an imbalance which places far too much reliance on public worship alone to feed us. To expect that one hour on Sunday morning can be sufficient for nurture of our spirits is naive, to say the least.

We are being faithful to our Reformed heritage when we recover the balance between public and private devotion by learning to cultivate privately the classic devotional practices of the Christian tradition.

Rejection of Sentimentality

The Reformed tradition has been suspicious about some forms of spirituality because of a deep-seated concern about the dangers of sentimentality. The insistence that our faith must make sense is a call for the serious exercise of the mind. Any spirituality that does not make full use of the intellect in the pursuit of truth is less than grateful to God for the gift of the mind. It is also likely to be irresponsible and unreliable.

Sentimentality is excessive emotionalism, which prefers feelings to careful thought. The emotions, by themselves, are not very reliable guides to the Christian. Feelings may come from an encounter with God or they may spring from our own neurotic needs.

Sentimentality takes a particularly modern form as a kind of self-indulgent narcissism whenever people wallow in pity for the less fortunate without doing anything to change the situation that makes them suffer. It also commonly expresses itself in an individualistic way in the expression "walk with Jesus," and makes that the goal and end of faith. It is not enough to have the right feelings unless these feelings lead us to thoughtful responses. Only a faith that is deeply rooted in the mind and is rigorous in the exercise of thinking can be obedient.

The Reformed rejection of sentimentality has meant turning away from those forms of piety which seek a warmhearted feeling and celebrate private feelings of intimacy with Jesus as the ultimate test of faithfulness. When piety degenerates into that kind of pietism, it wallows in feelings and uses emotions as a test for truth—if one *feels* right about Christ, then surely one *is* right. The emotions are made central as the means of receiving revelation. This leads to a misguided use of the imagination. People may, after all, commit terrible acts while feeling quite good about themselves at the time. They may even become so out of touch with reality that they believe God has commanded them to perform some terribly destructive act. The emotions can be dangerously misleading.

Yet the mind is not free from the dangers of being misled. Calvin, who treasured the gift of the mind as absolutely central to the definition of human, could also recognize the limitations of rationality. "For we know all too well by experience how often we fall despite our good intention. Our reason is overwhelmed by so many forms of deceptions, is subject to so many errors, dashes against so many obstacles, is caught in so many difficulties, that it is far from directing us aright."[15] Just as the emotions can mislead and distort our faith, so rationality can also be an escape from depth. Persons in the Reformed tradition need to be careful of trusting the mind too much. Too often we have made an idol of rationality.

Head knowledge needs the heart. The emotions cannot be left aside when we approach God. Edwards, seeking to understand and critique the powerful emotions set loose in the Great Awakening, makes the necessary connection between thought and feelings by using the analogy of heat and light: "There must be light in the understanding, as well as an affected fervent heart; where there is heat without light, there can be nothing divine or heavenly in that heart; so on the other hand, where there is a kind of light without heat, a head stored with notions and speculations, with a cold and unaffected heart, there can be nothing divine in that light."[16]

The unity of head and heart is focused in Calvin's definition of faith as "a firm and certain knowledge of God's benevolence toward us, founded upon the truth of the freely given promise in Christ, both revealed to our minds and sealed upon our hearts through the Holy Spirit."[17] Because faith involves truth as distinct from falsehood, it must include the mind. We understand what we believe or faith becomes meaningless nonsense. Yet rationality is not enough. By using the word "knowledge" Calvin does not mean "comprehension," but rather something beyond sense perception, which "is so far above sense that man's mind has to go beyond and rise above itself in order to attain it."[18] Head knowledge without the heart is not sufficient to persuade us and therefore move us to trust in God. Since trust is the heart of faith, the emotions must play a critical role in the exercise of faith. Calvin declares pointedly, "What help is it, in short, to know a God with whom we have nothing to do?"[19]

Reformed spirituality must have an intellectually objective character about it or it becomes dependent on our subjective response. But faith must not become limited to that which can be grasped with the mind or reduced to a verbal formula requiring intellectual assent. The Heidelberg Catechism defines true faith in a way that includes both elements:

> It is not only a certain knowledge by which I accept as true all that God has revealed to us in his Word, but also a whole-hearted trust which the Holy Spirit creates in me through the gospel, that, not only to others, but to me also God has given the forgiveness of sins, everlasting righteousness and salvation, out of sheer grace solely for the sake of Christ's saving work.[20]

The balance between heart and mind is critical. We must test our emotional experiences in the light of what we know, but, at the same time, knowledge without personal experience of the heart is a dead kind of knowing. One can be correct and still be without a relationship of trust with God. Thus knowledge and experience are the parallel necessities for the fullness of Christian faith, and united they prevent us from the false either/or of mind and heart.

Many of Calvin's followers who called themselves Calvinists were guilty of the divorce between faith as assent to correct doctrinal formulas and faith as a powerful emotional response to God's love which enables us to trust God in situations in which trust is very difficult. What has come to be known as salvation by faith has frequently been distorted into a teaching of salvation by right belief, and the

Christian life has been reduced to assent to the proper doctrines.

We, as Reformed Christians, are called to a rediscovery of the importance of faith as persuasion, as commitment, and as inner testimony or conviction, rather than as agreement or assent to a set of propositions. Such a rediscovery may enable us also to recover a balance between emotion and thinking and lead us to a spirituality that is not afraid of feelings.

Suspicion of Otherworldliness

Another characteristic of the Reformed tradition is the suspicion of any practice divorced from the world in which God has placed us. Christian faith has to do with the whole of life. There can be no separation between devotional practices of the Christian and the effect of these practices on one's business, family, and political life. Thus, any piety that seems to reject the physical world or that separates the world of the spirit from the world of flesh and blood is dangerous. Those forms of piety which treat creation as suspect or which disdain the world of politics and economics as beneath the concern of Christians are alien to the Reformed tradition.

There is no more serious distortion of biblical faith than that which makes a rigid distinction between flesh and spirit, especially when that division is also given value judgment so that flesh is bad and spirit is good. Many Christians have assumed that there is a world of the spirit which is free from the body, escapes the temptations of the flesh, and is, by the power of a disembodied risen Christ, enabled to avoid contamination with the stuff of this world.

Calvin struggled to free himself from that dichotomy. He rejected the common idea that sin came into the world by way of sensual temptation, and insisted that "unbelief has opened the door to ambition, but ambition has proved the parent of rebellion."[21] Ambition is not a sin of the flesh, but a sin of the mind and spirit. Sin is expressed in the totality of human life, thinking, feeling, action, politics, economics, and piety.

Because he rejected body-mind dualism, Calvin could celebrate the glory and beauty of nature as God's gift to human beings. "It is no small honour that God for our sake has so magnificently adorned the world, in order that we may not only be spectators of this beauteous theatre, but also enjoy the multiplied abundance and variety of good things which are presented to us in it."[22] This good creation is intended for human use as a gracious provision by a God whose liberality goes far beyond the need for survival. The world is filled with smells, tastes, and colors in rich abundance, and we are intended by their Creator to enjoy these sensual delights. Calvin described God's provision of food, "meant not only . . . for necessity but also for delight and good cheer." So also with clothing and other parts of creation. "In grasses, trees, and fruits, apart from their various uses, there is a beauty of appearance and pleasantness of odor,"[23] which are meant to be enjoyed. To reject or fail to appreciate the blessings of this life is to be ungrateful to the Giver, whose bounteous provision is for our enjoyment and use.

Because of a healthy worldliness within the Reformed tradition, the goal of the disciplines of the Spirit is not to remove us from the world, but to form us into the image of Christ so that we may become better equipped to act in the world as the people of God. All spiritual disciplines provide guidance and energy as we respond in faithfulness to the call of God in the place in which God has set us. Reformed guides for the spiritual life have insisted on the necessity of integration of piety with the way in which one lives out life in the world.

Calvin discarded the medieval monastic system of set-apart orders, not because he despised their practices or ideals, but because he wanted to break down the separation between holiness and life in the world. In the monastic world, a few people were set apart to live as all Christians were intended to live. He believed the monastic system had become a substitute for faithfulness on the part of the majority of Christians. In its severity toward the body, it also came dangerously close to a practice of glorifying the soul at the expense of the physical world. It appeared to seek life with God by rejecting life with other people. Calvin intended to integrate the disciplines of the spirit with the life of the whole people of God in the world.

Thus Calvin attacked the idea that the truly spiritual life could only be led by those who had given up the world and retreated into the monastic life. The ordinary Christian, living in the world, did not have to be content to benefit from the spirituality of the saints, whose merit they might appropriate but whose lives they could not really emulate. Calvin believed that the gospel "recommends to us the imitation of [Christ], for although we do not overtake him, it is yet meet that we should follow his steps, though at a distance."[24]

We must recognize that Calvin's attack can be justly accused of overstatement and caricature. He was, after all, on the defensive in what was a kind of holy war for the survival of the Reformation. It is nevertheless true that he was consistent in insisting that the contemplative life is not superior to a life of faithfulness lived with responsibilities for work, family, and community. The monastic hours were translated into the orders of morning and evening prayer for families. One could say that the ideal of Reformed Protestantism was that each Christian home become a little monastery in the world.

The Reformed tradition has the potential of providing strength and support for all people of God living out their lives in the world as those who have been set apart to their particular calling. Yet a weakness in the Reformed tradition has been that without the monastic system as an ideal to hold before all Christians, the tendency has been to become too easily adjusted to the particular culture of the time. It may be a sign of the need for balance in our tradition that the Taizé Community in France was begun by French, German, and Swiss Reformed Protestants, although it has become widely ecumenical. The life of the Iona Community in Scotland points to a similar need and response.

Potential for Renewal of Reformed Spirituality

There are three qualities that Calvin set forth as essential to the Christian life and always to be kept in balance. These three may provide the necessary points of creative tension to generate a lively spirituality among Reformed Protestants today. They are also in harmony with the spirituality of the historic faith of the church catholic expressed by Catherine of Genoa, Francis of Assisi, John of the Cross, Teresa of Avila, and a host of others.

Righteousness

One cannot be spiritual and live unjustly. "So when you are offering your gift at the altar, if you remember that your brother or sister has something against you, leave your gift there before the altar and go; first be reconciled to your brother or sister, and then come and offer your gift" (Matt. 5:23–24). Genuine spirituality cannot be had without paying the price of reconciliation with those who have something against us. It will work for justice in the world as an intrinsic part of its spiritual discipline.

Calvin insisted that the whole human race is bound together by God in a common fellowship. Within this fellowship, Calvin asserts, Christ so highly values the deeds of charity that "he will reckon as done to himself whatever we have bestowed on his people. . . . Christ is either neglected or honored in the person of those who need our assistance."[25] We are intended to grow in our relationship with neighbors as we grow in grace. Because neighbors include people we will never meet, the principle of justice must be at the heart of our spirituality so that we will not limit our concern to our immediate circle of friends or let it become privatized.

This insistence on the necessity for a spirituality that

includes our just relationships with others is one of the reasons Calvin so stridently argued against the practice of usury. Occasional instances of lending money to neighbors in need, for a modest return, he did not reject. But he had nothing good to say about those who make their living from lending money to others. They do not themselves contribute their labor to society. Unlike artisans, farmers, and merchants, moneylenders "sit at their ease without doing any thing, and receive tribute from the labour of all other people."[26] Lending money for interest also violates the principle of God's action in uniting all people in the bonds of mutual society, so that we may support and sustain each other. Among Christians especially, "it is required of the rich to succour the poor, and to offer bread to the hungry."[27] Justice toward other people is essential for any kind of relationship with God.

Frugality

Calvin's second mark of the Christian life has sometimes been called a "this-worldly" form of asceticism. Calvin insisted that the world is God's good gift to be enjoyed and cherished, but to cling to possessions, to cherish too much the comforts of the world, is to fall into idolatry. We must be ready to give up our possessions whenever they become so important that they have become idols.

Because we use our possessions to help or harm others, our attitude toward possessions is central for our spirituality. One of the classic features of Reformed piety is what Calvin called almsgiving. It is a discipline of the spiritual life to give sacrificially to those who are in need. Our response to human need actually opens us to receive God's grace. Calvin connected the giving of alms to prayers of intercession. Intercessory prayer is another way of assisting other people; in fact, it goes beyond what we can do materially for them. "Liberality of giving can be practiced only toward those whose poverty is visible to us. But we are free to help by prayer even utterly foreign and unknown persons, however great the distance which separates them from us."[28] It is impossible to pray for others without doing something about their need. Prayer and action thus belong together inseparably.

Fasting has an important place in Reformed spirituality as a correction of our natural tendency to greed and self-indulgence. Calvin ascribed a metaphorical meaning to fasting: "We do not understand it simply as restraint and abstemiousness in food, but as something else. Throughout its course, the life of the godly indeed ought to be tempered with frugality and sobriety, so that as far as possible it bears some resemblance to a fast."[29] Fasting represents the serious effort to avoid being so co-opted by our possessions that we are controlled by fear of losing them. Such a fear can easily lead to compromises with our faith. The Second Helvetic Confession states the connection between fasting and responsible gratitude to God:

> Now, the more seriously the Church of Christ condemns surfeiting, drunkenness, and all kinds of lust and intemperance, so much the more strongly does it commend to us Christian fasting. For fasting is nothing else than the abstinence and moderation of the godly, and a discipline, care and chastisement of our flesh undertaken as a necessity for a time being, whereby we are humbled before God, and we deprive the flesh of its fuel so that it may the more willingly and easily obey the Spirit.[30]

Fasting is also a particular and specific act in which we remove something from the normal routine of life, either for one day or for some other definite period of time. Within the Reformed tradition fasting has had three major purposes, as attested to by both Calvin and Lewis Bayly, writing over a century apart:

1. "We use it to weaken and subdue the flesh that it may not act wantonly," said Calvin,[31] to which Bayly adds the cautionary note that we do not fast "to weaken our Bodies, as that we are made unfit to do the necessary Duties of our Calling."[32] This use of fasting is one that makes us uncomfortable because it suggests that the flesh is somehow evil and opposed to the spirit. Perhaps we can understand this

purpose of fasting by seeing it as a matter of getting our priorities clear. To fast is to establish that food and drink are secondary to our loyalty to God.

2. We fast in order to prepare ourselves for prayer and meditation. Private fasting accompanies prayer as a means of enhancing our prayer. Calvin wrote about the fasting of Paul and Barnabas, saying that their purpose was to make them more eager and more unemcumbered for prayer. "Surely we experience this: with a full stomach our mind is not so lifted up to God that it can be drawn to prayer with a serious and ardent affection and persevere in it."[33] It is a very common human experience that fasting alters our mental state and changes our priorities. It may enhance and deepen our prayers.

3. We also fast "that it may be a testimony of our self-abasement before God when we wish to confess our guilt."[34] It can be either public or private. Public fasting is for the purpose of confessing corporate guilt and is a communal sign of repentance. In history it might have been either for the purpose of removing a public calamity or for obtaining a public blessing. The Puritans practiced such public fasts regularly, especially in the spring when seeds were buried in the earth. Spring was also a time of privation because the store of winter food supplies was nearly exhausted. It is an ironic coincidence that this spring fast of the Puritans corresponded in many ways to the rejected Roman Catholic observance of Lent.[35]

In spite of repeated insistence on the centrality of fasting as a support for prayer, the custom gradually fell into disuse among all American Protestants, including the Reformed. Jonathan Edwards was concerned about the lack of emphasis on fasting by the ministers of his time. He also connected fasting with private prayer:

> It is a duty recommended by our Savior to his followers, just in like manner as secret prayer is. . . . Though I do not suppose that secret fasting is to be practiced in a stated manner, and steady course, as secret prayer, yet it seems to me, it is a duty that all professing Christians should practice,

and frequently practice. There are many occasions, of both a spiritual and temporal nature, that do properly require it; and there are many particular mercies, that we desire for ourselves or friends, that it would be proper, in this manner, to seek of God.[36]

Since the time of Edwards, fasting has been neglected to the point where it has been forgotten that it ever was a discipline for Reformed Protestants. Most Protestants believe that fasting is a Roman Catholic practice, unless it has some utilitarian purpose such as weight loss or a political aim such as a demonstration of solidarity with oppressed and needy people. Our amnesia about fasting as a spiritual discipline may be related to our success in the economic sphere. Our material success has made us take for granted our abundance of possessions. The more possessions we have, the more difficult the discipline of fasting is to practice. We have become attached to our possessions and cannot bear the thought of doing without them.

Thus, fasting is the renunciation of an otherwise good thing. It is not a rejection of God's gifts, nor a demeaning of this world. It is not hatred of the body nor a belief that by punishing the body the soul can be enabled to grow or be purified. These attitudes presume a separation between body and soul which is unscriptural and un-Reformed.

Any recovery of authentic piety will need to consider carefully the place of fasting as a sign of frugality in the discipline of the Christian life.

Holiness

Holiness is that which unites us with Jesus Christ and thus makes us partakers in the blessings of the Holy Spirit within us. Justification by grace is not the end of the process of the Christian life. We are to grow in grace by the process that is called sanctification. The Christian is to mature, to live out a joyful and grateful life of response to what God has done. Even though we know that sin is always present with us, we are not to be content to wallow in our sin, but must move on and live as those who know the meaning of Christ for us.

Holiness is the fruit of the practice of the Christian life, so that we become aware of the indwelling of Christ. It is living with the mystery of that presence in and with us, which lifts us from coldness of heart and renews us and animates our faith. Calvin says, "That joining together of head and members, that indwelling of Christ in our hearts —in short, that mystical union—are accorded by us the highest degree of importance, so that Christ, having been made ours, makes us sharers with him in the gifts with which he has been endowed."[37]

This mystical union of the believer with Christ is the real heart of holiness in the Reformed tradition; it appears throughout Reformed literature and speaks powerfully of a sense of Christ living within us. Charles Hodge summarizes the doctrine of sanctification: "We are made holy not by the force of conscience, nor of moral motives, nor by acts of discipline, but by being united to Christ so as to become reconciled to God, and partakers of the Holy Ghost."[38]

Unlike some medieval forms of spirituality which spoke of union with God, Reformed spirituality has centered on union with Christ. Francis Rous, in the seventeenth century, who is probably the closest a Puritan ever came to being a mystic, described union with Christ, using the image of marriage, in these dramatic words: "Thou being married to him who is God, in him art also one with God. He one by a personal union, thou one by a mystical. And being thus united and married to him, his spirit flows into thy spirit, and the sap of the Deity sheds itself into thy soul."[39] He represents a Reformed mysticism at its best, passionately seeking union with Christ, knowing that such union is really a gift, but knowing also that it must be the goal of all waking activity.

These three characteristics—*righteousness, frugality,* and *holiness*—keep the Christian life in balance. Each is equally necessary for the wholeness of our faith and growth in grace. Righteousness keeps us aware of the duty of justice in the world. Frugality keeps us dependent on God's goodness and aware of the dangers of idolatry of possessions. And holiness is what unites us with Christ in mystical union and enables us to be strengthened to continue to live what may be a difficult life.

An authentic Reformed piety will have at least the following characteristics:

1. It will balance corporate and private devotion, so that the community of faith will be enriched by the practice of each one and the private lives of individuals will be corrected and deepened by the witness of the whole church.

2. It will balance emotion with thought, so that it is not merely sentimental but faithful. The scriptures will be central, and meditation and study of them will keep us honest about who our God really is. Yet, such study of scripture will not be coldly intellectual but will dare to experience the richness of the indwelling of Christ in the soul, the mystical union of the believer with Christ.

3. It will balance joyful acceptance of God's good world with a careful stewardship that does not get entangled in idolatrous clinging to possessions. It will practice the discipline of frugality, so that we do not become trapped by material possessions on the one hand, nor reject God's good gifts on the other.

4. It will balance the desire for quietness and relationship with God with a desire, animated by the presence of Christ, to live out our faith in service to others in the world. It will be a public as well as a private faith.

The key to understanding and practicing Reformed spirituality is to keep the tensions in balance. To fall off one side or the other is to become caught in dangerous excess. Richard Baxter spoke as a classic Calvinist and in his book *The Reformed Pastor* intended to provide a Reformed corrective to George Herbert's *Country Parson.* In *The Reformed Pastor,* he admonished his readers to observe four necessary qualities in their lives: prayer, study, conference, and practice.[40] These four practices maintained together will give the Christian life vitality without false or dangerous excesses. That is why Richard Baxter's simple advice is still important: *pray, study, confer,* and *practice.* Each of these is an essential mark of the Christian life, and together they keep us on balance.

> Grant, Almighty God, that as thou hast made known to us thy law, and hast also added thy gospel, in which thou callest us to thy service, and also invitest us with all kindness to partake of thy grace,—O grant, that we may not be deaf, either to thy command or to the promises of thy mercy, but render ourselves submissive to thee everywhere, and so learn to devote all our faculties to thee, that we may in truth avow that the rule of a holy and religious life, has been delivered to us in thy law, and that we may firmly adhere to thy promises, lest through any of the allurements of the world, or through the flatteries and delusions of Satan, thou shouldst suffer our minds to be drawn away from that love which thou hast once for all manifested to us in thine only-begotten Son, and in which thou daily confirmest us by the teaching of the gospel, until we at length shall come to the full enjoyment of this love in that celestial inheritance, which has been purchased for us by the blood of thine only Son. Amen.
>
> John Calvin[41]

NOTES

1. Presbyterian Church (U.S.A.), *The Book of Confessions* (New York and Atlanta: Office of the General Assembly, 1983), 4.021.

2. Gordon Wakefield, ed., *The Westminster Dictionary of Christian Spirituality* (Philadelphia: Westminster Press, 1983), p. 361.

3. John Calvin, *Institutes of the Christian Religion,* ed. John T. McNeill, trans. Ford Lewis Battles (Philadelphia: Westminster Press, 1960), I, II, 1, p. 41.

4. "Prayer, Religious Practices, and Sources for Christian Growth," *Presbyterian Panel,* March 1978, p. A-4.

5. *Book of Confessions,* 7.002.

6. Calvin, *Institutes,* III, XIX, 5, p. 837.

7. Emily Herman, *The Touch of God* (New York: George H. Doran, 1926), p. 18.

8. Calvin, *Institutes,* III, XI, 23, p. 753.

9. Samuel Rutherford, *Religious Letters* (Edinburgh and London: Anderson & Ferrier, 1894), p. 391.

10. Calvin, *Institutes,* IV, I, 5, p. 1018.

11. John Calvin, *Commentaries: The Book of Psalms,* trans. James Anderson (Grand Rapids: Baker Book House, 1984), 20:10, vol. 1, p. 343.

12. Calvin, *Institutes,* III, XX, 29, p. 892.

13. Presbyterian Church (U.S.A.), *Book of Order* (Louisville, Ky.: Office of the General Assembly, 1990), W-5.2000–.5000.

14. Calvin, *Institutes,* III, XX, 29, p. 892.

15. Calvin, *Institutes,* II, II, 25, p. 284.

16. Jonathan Edwards, *Religious Affections,* ed. John E. Smith, vol. 2, *The Works of Jonathan Edwards* (New Haven, Conn.: Yale University Press, 1959), p. 120.

17. Calvin, *Institutes,* III, II, 7, p. 551.

18. Calvin, *Institutes,* III, II, 14, p. 559.

19. Calvin, *Institutes,* I, II, 2, p. 41.

20. *Book of Confessions,* 4.021.

21. John Calvin, *Commentary on the First Book of Moses Called Genesis,* trans. John King (Grand Rapids: Wm. B. Eerdmans Publishing Co., 1984), 3:6, vol. 1, p. 153.

22. Calvin, *Commentaries: Psalms,* 104:31, vol. 4, p. 169.

23. Calvin, *Institutes,* III, X, 2, p. 720.

24. John Calvin, *Commentaries on the Catholic Epistles,* trans. and ed. John Owen (Grand Rapids: Baker Book House, 1984), 3:16, p. 219.

25. John Calvin, *Commentary on a Harmony of the Evangelists,* trans. William Pringle (Grand Rapids: Wm. B. Eerdmans Publishing Co., 1949), Matthew 25:40, vol. 3, p. 181.

26. Calvin, *Commentaries: Psalms,* 15:5, vol. 1, p. 213.

27. Calvin, *Commentaries: The Book of Ezekiel,* trans. Thomas Myers (Grand Rapids: Wm. B. Eerdmans Publishing Co., 1948), 18:5–9, vol. 2, p. 224.

28. Calvin, *Institutes,* III, XX, 39, p. 902.

29. Calvin, *Institutes,* IV, XII, 18, p. 1244.

30. *Book of Confessions,* 5.227.

31. Calvin, *Institutes,* IV, XII, 15, p. 1242.

32. Lewis Bayly, *The Practice of Piety* (London: Printed for Daniel Midwinter, at the Three Crowns, in St. Paul's Churchyard, 1714), p. 295.

33. Calvin, *Institutes,* IV, XII, 16, p. 1242.

34. Calvin, *Institutes,* IV, XII, 15, p. 1242.

35. Charles Hambrick-Stowe, *The Practice of Piety: Puritan Devotional Disciplines in Seventeenth-Century New England* (Chapel Hill, N.C.: University of North Carolina Press, 1982), p. 102.

36. Jonathan Edwards, "Thoughts on the Revival of Religion in New England," in *Edwards on Revivals* (New York: Dunning & Spaulding, 1832), p. 401.

37. Calvin, *Institutes,* III, XI, 10, p. 737.

38. Charles Hodge, *The Way of Life and Selected Writings,* ed. Mark A. Noll (Mahwah, N.J.: Paulist Press, 1987), p. 223.

39. Francis Rous, "The Mystical Marriage," from *Treatises and Meditations* (London: Robert White, 1657), p. 686.

40. Richard Baxter, *The Reformed Pastor* (New York: Robert Carter & Brothers, 1840), p. 77.

41. John Calvin, *Devotions and Prayers of John Calvin,* ed. Charles E. Edwards (Grand Rapids: Baker Book House, 1954), p. 65.

3

Prayer
in the Reformed Tradition

Q. Why is prayer necessary for Christians?
A. Because it is the chief part of the gratitude which God requires of us, and because God will give his grace and Holy Spirit only to those who sincerely beseech him in prayer without ceasing, and who thank him for these gifts.

The Heidelberg Catechism[1]

Prayer is a nearly universal human activity. From earliest times human beings sought ways to be in relationship with the mysterious and awesome powers that were of life-and-death importance for them. They tried to get in contact with these powers because these powerful forces that controlled the world in which they lived determined their very survival. Times of drought came, crops failed, and they went hungry. Outbreaks of disease wiped out whole communities, and it seemed that nothing could be done in the face of such disaster except to reach out and make contact with the god or gods, however dimly understood.

There is nothing uniquely Christian about prayer. Something inherent in the human spirit, when threatened by the unknown, cries out to whatever unseen powers there may be that seem to control the world. All prayer thus arises from the human sense of the transcendent, some power beyond what can be seen and touched. This sense of the beyond has led people in all times and places to try to come to terms with the mysterious, so that the powers may be inclined to be favorable toward us and make continued life possible and bearable.

It is natural for us all to pray to God for those things we need most. We try to get God to see things our way and to answer our requests favorably. We cannot and should not avoid such kinds of prayer. When we are in trouble we naturally cry out to God for safety, help, or relief from danger. There are many examples in scripture of prayer as an effort to get God to do something which a person or group needs. Prayers for rain, prayers for the success of armies in battle, prayers for the end of a pestilence, and prayers for long life and good health are common to all people.

In spite of our contemporary intellectual achievements, we have not outgrown our need for prayer as the effort to change the way things are. This "natural" prayer is so much a part of who we are as human beings that any approach to prayer that does not take it seriously is unrealistic. One of the reasons such "natural" prayer is important is that it is honest. We offer to God those needs which we feel most deeply. To withold anything from God because we think it selfish is to try to pretend before God. Calvin says that God "warns us and urges us to seek him in our every need, as children are wont to take refuge in the protection of the parents whenever they are troubled with any anxiety."[2] Thus our most genuine prayer begins with our sense of need.

Yet the very real and very dangerous temptation that faces everyone who prays is that of making prayer purely utilitarian. It easily becomes a means of asking God to provide what we seek, of trying to make God do our bidding. We may seek something for ourselves or for those we love. Our effort to get God to perform a miracle for us may be selfish or it may be completely altruistic. There is, however, an insidious risk in such an attitude; it causes us to be anxious. We cannot help wondering about the reliability of God. We cannot avoid the thought that God may not grant our requests, and fragile faith is threatened by the fear that our prayers may not succeed in producing the results we seek. We are either pleased by the results, if they are favorable, or deeply discouraged if they are not. We may measure the value of our prayers by the results. Thus, some people may continue to pray because their prayers seem to "work," and others give up the practice of prayer, except in moments of extreme crisis, because their prayers do not "work."

Because we live in an age in which results are the measure for the success of any and every venture, it is very tempting to view prayer as a way of getting concrete results. The fear that God will not give us what we really want hovers over all natural prayer. This seed of doubt may even keep people from prayer. They do not want to take the risk of having God let them down. At the same time, they know that they cannot live without some relationship with God. They would like to pray, but fear of failure keeps them from it; they are trapped in a dilemma and dissatisfied whichever way they choose to go.

One of the subtle attractions of books about prayer or workshops on prayer is that we may secretly hope that they will provide us with the clues as to how we may change our praying so that it will work more effectively for us. We hope that some new method will do for us what previous methods have not done. Even retreats or conferences on prayer may begin with this expectation lurking in the background, although often unspoken. Emily Herman calls our state one of "arrested development in prayer," and says that we have "to all practical intents and purposes, regarded prayer, in a deplorably mechanical way, as a process of importunate pleading and begging."[3] Yet even in our begging before God we indicate that we believe that God cares for us. Even when it is distorted, prayer is also a sign of trust; we beg God because we believe that God hears us. Such prayer does not have the luxury of being proper or correct, because it is too urgent. Natural prayer, however theologically stunted or self-centered it may be, is at least rooted in trust.

On the other hand, Christian prayer has some specific

dimensions that grow out of the model for prayer Jesus gave to the disciples and which we know as the Lord's Prayer. This prayer has the unique authority of the one whom we call our Lord and who thus sets the primary agenda for our own prayers. In the Lord's Prayer, the focus of attention is on God rather than on our own needs. The primary intent of the prayer is to seek after that which is in accord with God's will for us rather than to sway God's will to suit our purposes. We pray that God's name be hallowed, God's will be done, God's rule be realized on earth. Only then do we make modest requests for sufficient food for the day, for forgiveness that is contingent upon our willingness to forgive others, and for power to resist temptation. The prayer is one of willing abandonment of self to God's will.

In his great book on the subject, *A Method for Prayer,* Matthew Henry addresses the basic issue of the purpose of prayer in his introduction and declares, "Prayer is to move and oblige ourselves, not to move or oblige God."[4] His understanding of the purpose of prayer is not to make God understand us, for God already knows our inmost thoughts, but that we may better understand ourselves. Self-knowledge is a major benefit of prayer, but it is not a benefit that comes easily to people who are looking for easy answers to their problems from a God who does their bidding.

There is a radical difference between prayer as getting God to do our bidding and prayer as increased self-understanding and changing us to conform more nearly to God's will. If the one form of prayer is "universal" and "natural," the other form of prayer is "God-centered" and "relational." The purpose of the first is to get something, and the purpose of the second is to become something. Charles Hodge puts this distinction in stark terms by saying that prayer "is not simply petition, but converse with God."[5] In such conversation we seek, not merely to gain something from God, but to be in relationship with God. The goal is very different and the form that the prayer takes is also different. Instead of being a duty or an urgent expression of our need, prayer becomes an expression of what we believe about God and about ourselves.

Because he believed that prayer was at the very heart of the Christian life, John Calvin wrote extensively on the subject. His chapter on prayer in *Institutes of the Christian Religion* is one of the longest chapters in the whole work. From that chapter we can learn a great deal about what prayer has come to mean in the Reformed tradition. Calvin lists the reasons why we should pray. These reasons for prayer form a Reformed theology of prayer.

The Reasons for Prayer

The first reason is, in Calvin's words, "that our hearts may be fired with a zealous and burning desire ever to seek, love, and serve" God.[6] This reason for prayer, like that stated by Matthew Henry, has to do with the way we are changed by praying rather than with the way God is changed. Prayer is something that makes a difference in us. We pray in order to stimulate, deepen, and strengthen our faith.

This reason for prayer is almost a complete reversal of our usual idea, which is that we pray because our faith is strong and at its best. Prayer is an activity we are called to perform when our faith is not complete, when things are not going well, when God seems far from us. These are the times when we most need prayer. These are also the times when prayer is most difficult and we are prone to procrastinate in our praying, thinking that we just do not have enough time for prayer. We put off prayer and allow time for prayer to get squeezed out of our schedule even when we say to ourselves that prayer is vitally important to us. The near-universal difficulty of finding time for prayer on a regular basis suggests that more than laziness or lack of faith is the issue. We are up against some inner conflict about who we are and who God is, and our flight from prayer is also a way of fleeing from our confusion and ambiguity.

When we discover our resistance to prayer, we should realize that we are in deep conflict, whether we are conscious of it or not. Part of us wants to seek God's will and the other part of us is digging in its heels to resist. The resisting part of us finds excuses not to pray, becomes obsessed with the dry spells and bored with prayer. We begin to doubt that prayer is worthwhile or get distracted from prayer by a variety of fantasies. Richard Baxter was fully aware of these difficulties in his day: "The heart will prove the greatest hindrance in this heavenly employment; either by backwardness to it, or by trifling in it, or by frequent excursions to other objects, or by abruptly ending the work before it is well begun. As you value the comfort of this work, these dangerous evils must be faithfully resisted."[7] We need to pray most when we least want to do it, because our resistance is a sign of some spiritual problem that only manifests itself in our reluctance to pray.

The act of prayer is a way of renewing a sense of God's presence in our lives and of deepening our own faith. But such renewal and depth come only when we have resisted the temptation to give up and have pushed ourselves to the demanding work of prayer.

Secondly, Calvin says that we pray so "that there may enter our hearts no desire and no wish at all of which we should be ashamed to make [God] a witness."[8] Prayer requires that we think clearly about our wants and needs. We become so preoccupied with our own needs that they come to dominate and control our praying and we are unable to focus on God as the object of prayer. If we are ashamed to pray for something, then we had better reconsider our wanting of that thing. If we cannot bring a particular need before God, we may have to rediscover the appropriateness of that need. In God's presence, what we think we must have may change drastically. We have to get some distance from ourselves and from our unceasing wanting. Times of prayer may provide us with new clarity about ourselves. Prayer changes our wanting as we hold our wants before God.

Prayer is always closely related to self-examination. This

has been especially true in the Reformed tradition. Self-examination was part of each day's prayer for the Puritans; it formed a basis for the personal prayer of confession. In the same way, self-examination may be helpful for us today. It would force us to take a new look at who we are and to consider what we are doing with our lives. Self-knowledge enables us to be prepared for doubts, distractions, and temptations.

One of the reasons why persistence in prayer is so important is that it produces a change in us even when that change may be unwanted or undesired. It is one of the risks of prayer that we may find ourselves changed in ways that we do not expect. We may have our prejudices about other people turned around. One cannot, for example, continue to pray for another person and harbor a vengeful spirit toward that person. God works in us the miracle of a new perspective, when we might prefer to maintain our old attitude.

Third, Calvin says that we pray "that we be prepared to receive [God's] benefits with true gratitude of heart and thanksgiving."[9] As we look at our lives, we may not always find much to be thankful for. We may, in fact, be much more aware of the things that are wrong or lacking. It is a common human tendency to be more conscious of our troubles than of our blessings.

One great value in the discipline of prayer is that the very act of giving God thanks makes us take a second look at our lives and see in them the evidences of God's blessings. Baxter gives this advice:

> Reader, I intreat thee, remember this; let praises have a larger room in thy duties; keep matter ready at hand to feed thy praise, as well as matter for confession and petition. To this end, study the excellencies and goodness of the Lord as frequently as thy own wants and unworthiness, the mercies thou hast received and those which are promised as often as the sins thou hast committed.[10]

Prayers of thanksgiving enable us to take a look at what is going on in and around us from a consciousness that frees us from focus on the negative. Grateful prayer makes it possible for us to be thankful for the goodness of life in the midst of trouble. All of us might discover that the discipline of gratitude is a blessing. We would be enabled to see life as a wonderful gift and each day as a miraculous opportunity from God's loving providence. Prayer does not wipe away our troubles, but it does cause us to see them in relationship to our joys.

One of the greatest contributions of the prayer tradition in the black church is its emphasis on gratitude, often in the midst of terrible suffering. The frequently repeated positive exclamations such as, "Thank you, Jesus," and "Yes, Lord," are a common characteristic of black church prayer. This praise-filled prayer was a primary factor in giving black people hope in a situation that would otherwise be seen only as desperate. The black church as an institution has been a major force for preserving a sense of gratitude among black people, thus giving them power to ward off the hopelessness of bitterness and despair.

We all too easily take for granted the joys of life and are often barely conscious of them. We come to accept the good times as normal and our right. It is only when they are taken from us that we become aware of them by their absence. Our prayers of thanksgiving are a way in which we "obey grace," in the words of Karl Barth.[11] Thanksgiving is a way not of getting something from God but of recognizing God as the source of all that we are and have. It is a way of changing us by this acknowledgment. Those who regularly pray with thanksgiving do not take life for granted and are given the blessing of being able to see the gift in each day.

Fourth, Calvin says that, "having obtained what we were seeking, and being convinced that [God] has answered our prayers, we should be led to meditate upon his kindness more ardently."[12] Prayer changes our attitude toward God. As we pray, we come to see that God is the Divine Lover who hears our cries and whose will is for our wholeness and well-being.

It is not always easy to believe that we have obtained what we sought in prayer. We often speak about "unanswered prayer." God's answers to our prayers come in a variety of forms. Our task is to keep our eyes open so that we can recognize them when they take place. God's answer may take a form that is different from what we expected.

"No" is an answer to prayer. Parents are aware that saying no to a child is one way that we demonstrate our love for that child. The child is, of course, quite likely to see this answer as anything but an expression of love. Yet, as parents, we know that for the good of our children there are many times when we are required to respond to their ardent pleas with a negative. In the same way, we are children before God, the loving Divine Parent. It would be helpful for us to remember this truth in our own experience. Many prayers that we have all prayed have been answered negatively, and from the distance of time we have discovered that we were blessed by that divine "No!" If each one of us had received everything that we sought from God, we would be miserable creatures. Much that we ask for is selfish and of only very temporary value, at most. If our agenda for prayer is completely out of touch with God's agenda for us, we are unable to experience prayer as a blessing.

God also answers prayers with the demand for patience from us. The granting of a particular request may simply take more time than we wish, and it is an act of faith to wait patiently for God's response. Calvin acknowledges the frustration we all feel when prayers are not immediately answered. We begin to wonder about God, who "never either sleeps or idles, still very often gives the impression of one sleeping or idling in order that [God] may thus train us, otherwise idle and lazy, to seek, ask, and entreat [God] to our great good."[13]

Because prayer deepens faith, it changes our attitude from that of doubt or indifference toward God to one of hopefulness and expectation. To pray is to discover that God answers prayer in many different ways. Prayer prepares us to expect God's answers and to receive them in gratitude.

Calvin's reasons for prayer can assist us to see prayer as

relationship with God more than as pleading for what we want. His theology of prayer is God-centered and more concerned about how we may be shaped into the people God wills us to be than with how we may change God to fulfill our desires.

Our Problems with Prayer

It is hard to pray. All of us have problems with prayer. It is especially difficult to pray as citizens of a materialistic culture who live in a scientific age. Everything around us suggests that prayer is pointless. We are a people who want to believe that we can take care of ourselves. Prayer seems like an effort to avoid responsibility. We believe that we should act like adults, while prayer seems to reduce us to childishness. We have great difficulty believing in a God who makes a difference in a world that runs by natural laws, and prayer requires that we trust in God who is beyond natural law.

One of the greatest problems that contemporary Christians have with prayer is that we have forgotten who God is. We allow our ideas of God to be determined by images other than Christ, and thus fall into fear that God will reject us and our petitions. We consider that we are unworthy of prayer, that our lives are so stained that God can only condemn us. We may also believe that we are too unimportant for God to bother about. Our primary image of God may, in reality, be that of an unforgiving judge, who is to be feared far more than to be adored. Even though we may think we know better, that basic negative image of God working in our subconscious will prevent us from having enthusiasm about prayer. After all, who wants to get too close to a vengeful tyrant who may seek only to punish us.

Even though we may think that we have outgrown childish images of God, they may continue to operate in us and block us from prayer. Flora Wuellner, one of the most prolific and down-to-earth writers on the subject of prayer from within the Reformed tradition, writes this important advice: "Sometimes the deepest unfaced fear in the subconscious is . . . the fear of God . . . the very one whose love we know we need."[14] It is only as we allow Christ to reshape our image of God that we can move from a deeply held image of God as one to be feared to an image of God as one who can be approached without fear. Calvin acknowledged this situation, and recognized that our encounter with God may be one that inspires fear and drives us away from God until "Christ comes forward as intermediary, to change the throne of dreadful glory into the throne of grace."[15]

As we are reminded of God's graciousness in Christ Jesus, we are freed to be able to pray, because we know that the One to whom we pray is love. To pray in Christ's name is to be freed from the fear of God's righteous judgment and brought into awareness of our acceptance and forgiveness. Our image of God is changed by praying in Jesus' name. Karl Barth emphasizes the need to focus on Christ in prayer, declaring that in Christ all humanity is in the presence of God, so that as God knows us, sees us, and judges us, "it is always through the person of Jesus Christ."[16]

Our resistance to being in relationship with God is also the result of an overemphasis on the mystery and otherness of God. Within the Reformed tradition, the concern about the danger of idolatry has led to a consequent one-sided emphasis on God's transcendence. In order to insist that God may not be reduced to our level, there has been a tendency to forget the human dimension of God. This distorted view of God makes approach to such a God unappealing; it keeps us from prayer, or makes of our prayers an exercise of duty without much enthusiasm.

Prayer requires a relationship of trust with God. In order to pray with enthusiasm, we need to believe in a God who is personal, a God who cares about us individually and therefore invites our prayers. A powerful but distant God, who is far removed from the everyday concerns of human life, is not a God who inspires us to want to pray.

Unless we understand clearly that Christ stands with us in our weakness, shares our humanity, and stoops to lift us from where we are to the very presence of God, we will find that we continue to make excuses for our failure to pray regularly. So long as God seems far removed from us, our prayers will lack intimacy. Respect for both the transcendence of God and the intimacy of God in Christ is a necessary balance for us all.

Our view of God is frequently limited by our view of the natural world as absolute and unchangeable. Ever since the development, in the eighteenth century, of what has been called "the Enlightenment," we have held a faith in the power of the human mind. We have sought to understand and control nature and have believed, almost without question, that anything that could not be understood was not to be taken seriously. We have lived with a worldview that sees nature as operating according to fixed laws. Such a view of nature limits God and leads to the belief that prayer cannot make any difference. We lack trust that God can change the way things are. Only our concrete deeds can make a difference. It seems senseless to pray when any change can only come about by our own effort.

This unflexible and mechanistic attitude toward nature leads to the idea of our own indispensability. In a world of fixed laws, we had better do the best we can. We cannot depend on God, because even God can do nothing to change nature. Thus it is very difficult for us to let go of the idea of our self-importance and to trust that God can work without us, through us, or even in spite of us.

So long as we can cling to the notion that we are ultimately each in charge of our own life we do not really need God and we will not really want to pray. So long as we view our weakness as a disgrace, we will only pray in moments of extreme desperation.

Our desire to hold on to the facade of our own importance, our determination to take care of ourselves, and our need to be strong and independent are so deep-seated it may take a crisis in order for us to be broken open to a new view of our vulnerability. Dependence on God needs to be seen as openness rather than as weakness. We need God, not because we are unable to care for ourselves, but because we were created for such a relationship. To be closed up in ourselves, pretending that we are self-sufficient, is really to live dishonestly, for it denies part of our human nature. All of us know ourselves well enough to see our limitations and weaknesses. Honesty about ourselves requires that we let go of the false idea of our self-sufficiency.

Prayer is an act of letting go. It is not one more activity among other activities. To pray is to do nothing. We set aside the many things that we could be doing and, for a time at least, we trust that God will continue to work in the world without our direct and concrete actions. Prayer requires time, and we are slaves to the clock and the calendar. We tend to measure our lives in terms of work accomplished. Only when we believe that prayer is important will we make the necessary time available. In this sense, finding time for prayer is like making time for the Sabbath. In both cases we are required to let go of the need to be productive. In our busy world, prayer is extremely difficult. Yet without taking the time our faith is weakened, and we are weaned away from that which we claim is central in our lives. Baxter says that "to prevent a shyness between God and thy soul," it is necessary to pray regularly and frequently. "The chief end of this duty is to have acquaintance and fellowship with God, and therefore if thou come but seldom to it, thou wilt keep thyself a stranger still."[17]

The chief hindrances to prayer in the twentieth century are distorted images of God which cause us to avoid companionship with God and distorted images of ourselves which cause us to seek to prove our own self-sufficiency by trying to go it alone. A recovery of a Christological focus for our image of God and a recovery of a sense of our need for God in order for us to be fully human are both a deep part of our Reformed heritage.

The Recovery of Balance in Prayer

There are four necessary balances in prayer, which are essential for us to remember if we are to recover a lively and meaningful style of prayer. They are rooted in our tradition as Reformed Christians. Each of these is a way of maintaining the necessary tension in prayer, which prevents us from falling into the trap of excess, of idolatry, or of privatism.

1. Prayer is both corporate and personal. We pray alone because we also pray with others and we pray with others because we have a private prayer discipline which enriches our corporate praying. Prayer with others is a way to learn a great deal about ourselves and them. We may be taught by others what to avoid or be careful about in our private prayers. We may also be taught to widen our horizons by the concerns of others in the community of faith. Private prayer without public prayer can become so personal that it shuts out concern for the world beyond our touch. Thus corporate prayer is a corrective to private prayer; it prevents it from becoming self-centered.

But if we bring no private experience to public prayer, we shall find ourselves empty and our corporate prayers may become dull and meaningless. Jesus not only prayed with his disciples but he went apart to be alone with God. He gave us insight about our own need for solitariness by his example.

2. Prayer is both spontaneous and disciplined. A good prayer book that contains the great prayers of the ages is an excellent tool to stimulate private prayer. It may also assist us through the dry times when spontaneous prayer is most difficult. The prayers of others act as a guide for our reflection. It is interesting to note that while the Puritans did not approve of the use of read or memorized prayers in public worship, their manuals for private devotion included sample prayers which they were encouraged to use. The prayers of others can deepen our own prayers. They can help us to pray when we cannot find the words ourselves.

Finally, however, our prayers need to become our own. Spontaneous prayer is just that—it is the prayer that comes from within as we discover that we are led to offer to God parts of our lives, which no one else can do for us. Spontaneous prayer need not be correct or beautifully phrased; because it belongs to us alone, its primary requirement is that it be immediate and intimate.

3. Prayer is an affair of the mind and the heart. Prayer needs to be both intellectual and emotional. God gave us minds, and the Reformed tradition has cherished this gift, but at the same time prayer needs to be a matter of the heart if it is to be a way of being open to God. No one ever accused Karl Barth of anti-intellectualism, yet he declared: "Prayer must be an act of affection; it is more than a question of using the lips, for God asks the allegiance of our hearts. If the heart is not in it, if it is only a form which is carried out more or less correctly, what is it then? Nothing!"[18] God welcomes our feelings as much as our thoughts, and we need to allow our fear of those feelings to fall away so that we can be accessible to the power of God. We bring to God our deepest longings, sometimes without words; thus prayer includes both laughter and tears.

4. We need to pray as both speakers and hearers. We speak to the Other and we listen for the Other to address us. We offer our words to God, for they express our honest needs and concerns; but, at the same time, prayer involves listening for God in an attitude of receptivity. This means that prayer that is balanced and healthy will involve periods of expectant silence as well as periods of passionate speech.

In order to get beyond the din of our culture and its impulsive character, we need to free ourselves from the drive for success and accomplishment that dominates and controls us even within the church. Prayer in which we stop talking and are quietly attentive to God is difficult, for it requires that we let go of our agenda. For such prayer we must lay down our old selves and accept a new self which is at some distance from the world. Only thus can we face that world as those who see it from a new perspective, which comes from the living Christ. Dorothee Soelle, a contemporary German theologian, describes a variety of religious practices which all have a way of stretching us so we are "standing somewhat apart from the outer world which is so deeply ingrained in us."[19] She says that when we meditate, for example, we are not withdrawing from reality, but "we are assuming another relationship to reality, one of wholeness, in which the selection dictated by our interests is shorn of its power."[20] In this sense, listening prayer is a radical act, and those who pray are enabled by their very distance from cultural captivity to see with new eyes what is otherwise obscured or hidden from them.

One of the reasons that prayer often seems unreal today is that we seem unable to acknowledge our participation in evil. In our concern to avoid negative feelings about ourselves, we see any admission of personal sin as a sign of a low self-image. We are reluctant to admit our weaknesses because we are not convinced of our own worth. We prop ourselves up with half-truths and outright lies in the effort to sustain our sense that we are acceptable. Not only does this effort exhaust us, it also keeps us from discovering our hope in God's pardon. We cannot be healed from what we have not exposed to the light. Reformed prayers may seem overly negative about life, but just such integrity is a beginning place for us for recovery of prayer.

The reflections of Elizabeth Singer Rowe in her journal are typical of the negative self-assessment in many Puritan prayers: "Break, break, insensible heart! let confusion cover me, and darkness black as my own guilt, surround me. Lord, what a monster am I become! How hateful to myself for offending thee!"[21] Yet she is able to engage in such abject confession because she also believes in her pardon: "By titles of the most tender import thou hast made thyself known to my soul: titles which thou dost not yet disdain, but art still compassionate, and ready to pardon."[22]

In dramatic contrast to our contemporary tendency toward making excuses for our sins, our ancestors in faith were tough-minded, severe on themselves, and ardent in their confessions. At least once each day, they got down on their knees and reflected on the day, on those things which they had done wrong, on those whom they had wronged, on that which they had neglected to do, and they opened themselves to the mercy of God and the healing of God's forgiving love. We are much more likely to let our guilt and self-hate simmer within us, unexpressed and unhealed. A healthy recovery of confession and self-examination might very well be a source of mental health. It would also make our prayers honest.

Prayer in the Reformed tradition is strongly confessional in character. The corporate prayer of confession is a central part of all Reformed liturgies, and in private prayer confession is closely linked to self-examination. Confession also requires belief in God's forgiveness. Without such trust we do not dare to acknowledge our failures; we hold back out of fear of condemnation. In public prayer, the assurance of pardon is an essential ingredient to enable us to confess without hesitation.

Perhaps the most essential requirement for a lively recovery of prayer today is the practice of solitude. It is hard to get away from other people, from noise, and from the press of events in our kind of world. We are so accustomed to words that we use noise as a vehicle for escaping nagging thoughts and troublesome feelings, which we prefer to repress in order to maintain the facade of ourselves that we want to preserve.

Prayer requires solitude. We need to have times when we are alone and can bring the depth of ourselves into the presence of God. Baxter advises, "Retire into some secret place, at a time the most convenient to thyself, and laying aside all worldly thoughts, with all possible seriousness and reverence, look up toward heaven."[23] In solitude and privacy we can express those things we dare not speak of in the presence of any other person. We can expose and acknowledge those parts of ourselves of which we are most ashamed, and we can express the deepest longings of our hearts without concern about what others will think. The Reformed tradition has consistently argued for the necessity of privacy in prayer.

It is sometimes difficult for us to distinguish the aloneness of solitude from simple loneliness. Loneliness is feeling incomplete and longing for a relationship that has been broken or denied or has never existed. Loneliness is a painful curse, and our fear of loneliness drives us to seek to escape being alone. We call friends, we plan activities, we

turn on the television set, all in the anxious effort to avoid
loneliness. Solitude, on the other hand, is something to be
sought after. It is an attitude of the heart and a willingness
to lay ourselves open to God. As such it "does not depend
on physical isolation."[24] Solitude can be found in the midst
of noise and activity if we can learn how to practice the art
of inner quiet.

Quiet does not come about naturally for most of us. We
must learn how to be quiet, and this is not easy. Even when
we have closed the windows, unplugged the phone, and are
without external distractions, we may still be filled with
inner noise, with dreams and plans and other intrusions
that fill our minds. The psalmist understood our need for
silence: "Be still, and know that I am God" (Ps. 46:10). The
noise within us is a block to our receptivity to the work of
God in our lives. There is a kind of knowing that can take
place only when we put aside the noise, including the noise
of words, and are simply quietly open and receptive. Then,
and only then, we discover God's presence as a personal
reality for us.

It takes courage to be both alone and silent. We do not
know what to expect and are not in a position to exercise
control. We are so accustomed to busy activity that we run
as if to escape from God. Inner quiet is a way of coming
into the awareness of the presence of God by leaving behind
our very full agendas. It is a way of emptying ourselves so
that God can fill us.

As we become quiet, we discover that prayer does not
require words. Calvin says that "the best prayers are
sometimes unspoken."[25] The Puritans developed the practice of what they termed "extraordinary prayer" as distinct
from regular or "ordinary" prayer, which took place at set
times during the day. They suggested phrases or words
upon which to fix one's attention when praying, by repeating the name "Jesus," or the word "love," over and over.
They even suggested that inward sighs and groans might be
sufficient.[26] The terms "meditation" and "mental prayer"
were used to point to prayer that does not use words. The
Reformed tradition has maintained the practice of contem-

plative prayer, although it has often been forgotten along-side the very strong insistence that prayer must be in carefully thought-out words and phrases.

If we really seek depth in our relationship with God, we may need to begin to practice the discipline of waiting in silence. Prayer as monologue is not really conversation. Our ceaseless words may even make our prayers a shield to keep God out. So long as we do the talking, we are in control. Baxter advises us that we need to prepare for prayer by a conscious act of self-emptying. He says, "Get thy heart as clear from the world as thou canst. Wholly lay by the thoughts of thy business, troubles, enjoyments and everything that may take up any room in thy soul. Get it as empty as thou possibly canst that it may be the more capable of being filled with God."[27]

Silent prayer involves us in attitudes of listening, waiting, and paying attention to God. Such prayer is surrendering our words and therefore our will for periods of time, just to be in the presence of God. This is hard work, and no one should minimize the difficulty. We need ways of developing the discipline of silence in our own lives. Such practices will assist us in turning off the flow of noise from within. The great Puritan divines suggested that we use passages of scripture as guides for keeping our attention fixed on God. They also used pictures of biblical scenes which were carefully engraved in their Bibles and prayer books. These pictures enabled the mind to concentrate on the events depicted and allow the imagination to enliven them so that the believer could become part of the biblical story.

Meditation does not necessarily mean being empty of any images, words, or ideas. Into a mind that has gone blank there is no assurance as to what may come. In order to make certain that the meditation is fixed on God, we do well to follow the example of our ancestors in faith and concentrate on scripture, biblical scenes, or words of faith.

The risk of being quiet is that we may become very uncomfortable. Without the comforting distraction of noise and activity, we may discover much that we would rather not know about ourselves. We may be aware of unresolved anger, of festering resentment, or of persistent temptation we thought we had gotten rid of. Quiet may be disconcerting. Yet this inner quiet with all its discomfort is a necessity if we are to discover the fullness of God's presence with us.

In order to engage in any form of meditation we must be prepared to face the darkness in ourselves. We may be forced to admit our anger at God and express it. So long as it is buried, it will never do anything but eat away at us from inside. The psalms are a very helpful guide for this. They help us to acknowledge our true feelings, especially when these feelings are not acceptable to us. Most of us were brought up to believe that nice people, and especially Christians, do not have feelings of anger and resentment. When we have these feelings, therefore, we are strongly tempted to deny them, to pretend that they are not real, or to ignore them.

In the state of inner quietness we are able to respond with tenderness to our own internal noises. We can acknowledge our repressed anger and resentment without letting the emotions trap us. We can discover the inner quiet that is able to simply be in expectation and thus be receptive to what God gives. Sometimes that waiting can seem a desert place, and we may wish to flee from the sense of God's absence.

Thus, Reformed spirituality is fully conscious of the struggle of the "dark night." In its realism, it is in harmony with Saint John of the Cross and others in the tradition of the Roman Catholic Church who struggled through the pain of God's absence. It knows and respects that prayer may not produce experiences of fullness or even of God's presence. There are times when it is important to pray when we have no sense of any presence of God at all.

Yet Reformed spirituality is not content to remain in darkness without doing anything, for this can only lead to despair and neglect of the duties one owes to others. Francis Rous, after describing at length the experience of the absence of Christ in his own life, urges his readers not to use such occasions as temptations to despair or to give up. He reminds us that in such times we are bewildered and do not know what to do. He then advises:

> Thy most ordinary work, is the work of thy ordinary calling; yet mayest thou give times and turns to those works that more immediately concern thy heavenly calling even such as immediately call for thy heavenly Lord to come into thy soul: sigh and pray, and read and hear, and by heavenly meditations let thy soul be trimmed as a bride that looks for her husband; yea, with thy earthly labours, mayest thou mix these heavenly thoughts.[28]

This practical mix of the regular pursuit of the ordinary tasks of life with the special labors of private devotion is a healthy prescription for us all when we experience our own sense of desolation and absence.

No regular pattern of private prayer develops by itself. It requires effort, time, patience, courage, faith, and the encouragement of other Christians. Calvin is very explicit about the necessity of regular hours for prayer, but not "as if paying our debt to God, we imagine ourselves paid up for the remaining hours. Rather, it must be a tutelage for our weakness, which should be thus exercised and repeatedly stimulated."[29] Baxter gives careful advice about choosing the best time of the day for regular prayer:

> Choose also the most seasonable time. All things are beautiful and excellent in their season. Unseasonableness may lose the fruit of thy labour, may raise difficulties in the work, and may turn a duty to a sin. The same hour may be seasonable to one and unseasonable to another. . . . Such as can choose what time of the day they will should observe when they find their spirits most active and fit for contemplation and fix upon that as the stated time. I have always found that the fittest time for myself is the evening, from sun-setting to the twilight.[30]

The need for regularity and habit in prayer is to protect us from our own avoidance of prayer, our laziness and hesitation to pray. Without a carefully developed habit, we will not find time to pray; we will allow the activities of life to crowd out the time we had set aside for prayer; we will discover that we are just too tired or not in the right mood for prayer.

The results of regular prayer are not always those we may seek. We may not find instant peace or have grand visions or discover that we have immediate clarity about ourselves or even that we are freed from those parts of ourselves that we wish were removed from us. We pray with the promise that God does hear us, that God wills to be in relationship with us, that life without God is less than it was meant to be. We pray because God stooped to our condition in Jesus Christ to invite us into a living relationship. Our prayers are our saying yes to the great invitation to live, not alone, not in the darkness and anxiety of our self-seeking, but in and with and through the One who made us, who seeks us when we would flee, who loves us when we are hateful to ourselves, and who forgives what we cannot. This One slowly but surely molds us and fashions us into the image of Jesus Christ.

> Almighty God, forgive my diffidence, while I confess it is most inexcusable.—Thy hand is not shortened, nor are the springs of thy bounty sealed; thy ancient miracles have not exhausted thy strength, nor hath perpetual beneficence impoverished thee; thy power remains undiminished, and thy mercy endureth for ever. That dazzling attribute surrounds me with transporting glories: which way soever I turn, I meet the bright conviction; I cannot recall a day of my past life on which some signature of thy goodness is not stamped.
>
> Elizabeth Rowe[31]

NOTES

1. Presbyterian Church (U.S.A.), *The Book of Confessions* (New York and Atlanta: Office of the General Assembly, 1983), 4.116.

2. John Calvin, *Institutes of the Christian Religion,* ed. John T. McNeill, trans. Ford Lewis Battles (Philadelphia: Westminster Press, 1960), III, XX, 34, p. 897.

3. Emily Herman, *Creative Prayer* (New York: Harper & Brothers, 1934), pp. 17–18.

4. Matthew Henry, *A Method of Prayer* (Philadelphia: Presbyterian Board of Publication, n.d.), p. vi.

5. Charles Hodge, "Conference Papers," in *Charles Hodge: Selected Writings,* ed. Mark Noll (New York: Paulist Press, 1987), p. 257.

6. Calvin, *Institutes,* III, XX, 3, p. 852.

7. Richard Baxter, *The Saints' Everlasting Rest* (New York: Doubleday & Co., 1978), p. 169.

8. Calvin, *Institutes,* III, XX, 3, p. 852.

9. Calvin, *Institutes,* III, XX, 3, p. 852.

10. Baxter, *Saints' Everlasting Rest,* p. 127.

11. Karl Barth, *Prayer According to the Catechisms of the Reformation: Stenographic Records of Three Seminars,* adapt. A. Roulin, trans. Sara F. Terrien (Philadelphia: Westminster Press, 1952), p. 26.

12. Calvin, *Institutes,* III, XX, 3, p. 852.

13. Calvin, *Institutes,* III, XX, 3, p. 853.

14. Flora Slosson Wuellner, *On the Road to Spiritual Wholeness* (Nashville: Abingdon Press, 1978), p. 52.

15. Calvin, *Institutes,* III, XX, 17, p. 875.

16. Barth, *Prayer,* p. 22.

17. Baxter, *Saints' Everlasting Rest,* p. 134.

18. Barth, *Prayer,* p. 27.

19. Dorothee Soelle, *Death by Bread Alone: Texts and Reflections on Religious Experience,* trans. David L. Scheidt (Philadelphia: Fortress Press, 1978), p. 73.

20. Soelle, *Death by Bread Alone,* p. 79.

21. Elizabeth Singer Rowe, *Devout Exercises of the Heart,* ed. Isaac Watts (Baltimore: J. Kingston, 1811), p. 120.

22. Rowe, *Devout Exercises of the Heart,* p. 124.

23. Baxter, *Saints' Everlasting Rest,* p. 173.

24. Henri J. M. Nouwen, *Reaching Out: The Three Movements of the Spiritual Life* (Garden City, N.Y.: Doubleday & Company, 1975), p. 25.

25. Calvin, *Institutes,* III, XX, 33, p. 897.

26. Charles Hambrick-Stowe, *The Practice of Piety: Puritan Devotional Disciplines in Seventeenth-Century New England* (Chapel Hill, N.C.: University of North Carolina Press, 1982), pp. 164, 185.

27. Baxter, *Saints' Everlasting Rest,* p. 140.

28. Francis Rous, "The Mystical Marriage," from *Treatises and Meditations* (London: Robert White, 1657), pp. 709–10.

29. Calvin, *Institutes,* III, XX, 50, p. 918.

30. Baxter, *Saints' Everlasting Rest,* p. 135.

31. Rowe, *Devout Exercises of the Heart,* p. 163.

4

Study: The Uses
of the Bible
in Reformed Spirituality

Q. How is the Word to be read and heard, that it may become effectual to salvation?

A. That the Word may become effectual to salvation we must attend thereunto with diligence, preparation, and prayer; receive it with faith and love; lay it up in our hearts; and practice it in our lives.

The Westminster Shorter Catechism[1]

Scripture has always been central in the lives of Reformed Christians. They have rightly been called a people of the Book. The language of the Bible has shaped prayers within the Reformed tradition, biblical images have been the chief inspiration for its hymnody, its exposition has been the central focus of its worship. Richard Baxter's insistence on study as a mark of the Christian life means, above all, the study of scripture. Reformed piety is characterized by a strenuous and serious attention to the Bible as the source and guide for the spiritual life.

One reason for this high role for scripture is the concern of Reformed Christians about the danger of idolatry. The Heidelberg Catechism describes idolatry: "It is to imagine or possess something in which to put one's trust in place of or beside the one true God who has revealed himself in his Word."[2] Our tendency to replace God with some other goal

or good in our lives is so universal that we need to be
suspicious of ourselves and cautious about those things
which become too important to us. We cannot trust either
our minds or our feelings to give us reliable instruction
about the Christian faith and life. Without some trustwor-
thy standard by which to measure ourselves and our faith,
we may very well begin to worship an idolatrous god of our
own making. It has been an article of faith among Reformed Christians that only the Bible can keep us honest in
our faith and our prayers. Thus, the use of scripture as a
guide for reflection and prayer is a major emphasis in the
Reformed tradition.

Unless our meditations and prayers are directed toward
the God who is revealed in scripture, we will develop a
spirituality that is essentially idolatrous and devoid of
Christian content. In a masterpiece of Puritan spiritual
writing, Lewis Bayly lists seven "Hindrances, which keep
back a sinner from the practice of piety," and the first of
these hindrances is "an ignorant mistaking of the true
meaning of certain places of the holy Scripture."[3] He
describes how easily we distort the meaning of scripture to
suit our own purposes and how essential it is, therefore,
that Christians be well instructed in scripture. He is faithfully following Calvin, who warned about how necessary it
is for Christians to be constantly corrected by the Word,
"being aware of their own weakness, nothing better is left
for them but to keep themselves carefully within the limits
of God's Word, lest, if they wander far according to their
own predilection, they stray quite out of the right way,
insomuch as they are void of that Spirit by whose teaching
alone truth is distinguished from falsehood."[4]

Whether for the corporate community of the church or
for individuals reflecting by themselves, the Bible can keep
us honest and faithful. When it is used responsibly and
carefully, the Bible functions in the life of the church and in
the life of the individual believer to nurture, criticize, and
reform that life. The very name "Reformed" means to be
reformed by the Word of God.

Without a studious and well informed use of the Bible,

the individual Christian cannot be kept from idolatry, superstition, or following the latest cultural trends. It is very easy to become completely captive to the particular culture in which we find ourselves. The inspired character of scripture may be experienced in its supracultural character. Scripture has the unique ability to speak with authority in many different cultural settings. Of course, we must read it with great care to enable this to happen. It is quite possible for people to read the Bible without any effort to make the translation from the culture in which it was written, and therefore to try to apply its words directly to their own culture. Tragic distortions of scripture are the result of such a way of reading. It is also possible to hear in such a way that the great cultural gap between the authors and ourselves as readers is overcome and we can hear a meaningful word addressed to us. That is why the use of scripture is so very important for the Christian life.

In addition, it needs to be said that reflective reading of scripture in the late twentieth century is not easy. A major problem that most people have with the Bible today is that they are not sure that it can be trusted. To read the Bible is to be confronted by a culture that is vastly different from our own. It is thoroughly patriarchal, which means that reading large parts of it can be very painful for most women and many men. It has passages that are militaristic in the extreme, even demanding total slaughter of all the people in a vanquished town. At times it appears to defend slavery, describes polygamy without clear condemnation, and commends severity in the treatment of children. At other times it condemns divorce and lending money for interest without exception. Many passages appear to see childlessness, infant mortality, and all forms of human sickness as forms of divine punishment for sin. What do we make of these passages? How do they speak to us in our culture? Because we believe we lack handles on the answers to these important questions, many people are afraid of the Bible and do not use it for their spiritual enrichment.

Most people who do not have the scholarly tools of the biblical/critical scholar may be tempted to give up on the

Bible. They are likely to think that they do not know
enough to read it intelligently, and so leave it to the experts.
There is a gap between the pulpit and the pew, because
pastors are, by and large, trained in scholarly methods of
study. Walter Wink, among many contemporary biblical
scholars, is critical of the way that the scholarly community
has maintained its authority over scripture and suggests
that, while there will always be a role for the work of the
scholar, there are other ways to interpret that are equally
faithful, such as situations of personal suffering or social
alienation in which the reader has been freed from the
cultural captivity of the text and may be able to read it as
accurately as the scholar. "Biblical scholars must resist the
temptation of establishing themselves as scribal mandarins
jealously pocketing the keys of knowledge. And the oppressed and non-expert must avoid the temptation of
anti-intellectualism and that form of 'pneumatic exegesis'
which simply reads off the text what one already thinks he
[or she] knows."[5] The real problem is that most people in
the pew and many pastors do not believe that they have the
skills necessary to read the text, and because they demean
their abilities, they are afraid of the Bible.

There are several ways in which contemporary Christians
respond to their particular doubts and struggles with the
Bible today. All of them are efforts to hang on to some use
of the Bible without much confidence that either the Bible
itself or one's ability to read it can be trusted.

One is to ignore biblical scholarship and to use passages
as proof texts or slogans to support previously held positions. This is an easy way to use scripture, although it is not
very responsible and tends to reinforce already held ideas
rather than to discover God's surprising truth. Such proof
texts are used to defend ideas from attack rather than to
discover a word from God. The danger of this is that people
can make the Bible defend almost any practice. In the name
of following the lead of scripture, they can feel comfortable
defending their actions against any challenge.

Another is to develop a "canon within the canon." We all
do this by collecting a few favorite texts which do not

trouble us, which comfort us and give us a sense of God's love for us, and which by frequent use become our real scripture. We ignore the rest of the Bible, by and large. Although this method may strengthen faith in times of trial, it does not subject a person to the sometimes harsh demands of God or unpleasant realities about the life of a disciple that may be hidden in those parts of scripture which are ignored.

A third way is to psychologize the text so that we ask only how the text makes us feel or what it tells us about our inner life. While this is one legitimate way of asking questions of the text, when it becomes the only way we approach the Bible we have really adopted a new kind of allegorical method. The actual stories lose their importance, and the Bible ceases to be the authoritative source of our faith. Instead of revealing God to us, the Bible becomes a way we analyze ourselves. We lose the critical distance between ourselves and the text.

Reformed Biblical Interpretation

Because we take the Bible so seriously, it is only natural that Reformed Christians have had many heated debates about biblical interpretation. Nearly every major conflict within the churches of this tradition has been rooted in the principle of proper interpretation of scripture. Each side claims that it has the truth because it alone correctly understands the Bible.

Calvin and the other Reformers were aware of the problems of interpretation. They were products of the complicated methods of biblical interpretation that were common in the late Middle Ages. There were at least four established methods of interpreting any biblical image: (1) the historical or literal meaning of the text, (2) the allegorical meaning, (3) the eschatological or final meaning for the end of time, and (4) the moral or personal meaning. Thus the Temple of the Lord could refer (1) to the building in Jerusalem where the Hebrew people most clearly found God, (2) to Jesus as the presence of God among people, (3) to the New Jerusalem (the whole city was to be filled with God's presence, and so no specific temple was to be needed), and (4) to the Christ present in us. Pre-Reformation preaching tended to follow the allegorical method and to reject the literal meaning as dead or meaningless. The Reformers broke free from allegorical interpretation and insisted on the literal, or natural, meaning of the text. Calvin attacked allegory with biting irony as an excuse for playing games with "the sacred word of God, as if it had been a ball to be tossed to and fro."[6] He thought it essential to avoid such games, because the plain meaning of the text is sufficient. We must not think "that, under the outer bark of the letter, there lurk deeper mysteries, which cannot be extracted but by beating out allegories."[7]

Calvin understood scripture as God's accommodation to human limitations. "For who even of slight intelligence does not understand that, as nurses commonly do with infants, God is wont in a measure to 'lisp' in speaking to us?"[8] This accommodation to us includes the use of expressions that must not be taken literally. The limitation of human language is that it can be crude, as when it ascribes to God a mouth, ears, eyes, and so on, but it is the vehicle that God uses in a process of adjusting language to our human capacity so that we can hear and understand. Many of the passages that cause the most trouble for contemporary Christians might be more easily and clearly understood by following Calvin on this matter. They are part of the necessary accommodation to the limitations of human language.

Because he appreciated the limitations of human language, Calvin sought to avoid the trap of fixing the meaning of the Word of God in the specific words of the text itself. He could be quite critical of particular texts, finding errors or disagreeing with what is said. Although he did not always succeed in his effort to preserve the distinction between the Word and words, he maintained that the inner testimony of the Holy Spirit is essential if the Word is to have any meaning or power for us.

Our experience as readers is of this inner testimony of the

Spirit, which alone enables the Word to find a place in our hearts. Without the work of the Spirit, the Word gets reduced to words that may or may not have any connection with our lives. The distinction between the living Word enlivened by the power of the Spirit and the literal word is one that is delicately preserved in Calvin as a guard against what he saw as two extremes. On the one hand, he rejected the rationalistic scholasticism that demanded proofs prior to faith in scripture, and on the other, he strongly rejected the sectarians who claimed leadings of the Spirit apart from and even contrary to scripture.[9]

Calvin believed that it was possible to read scripture without understanding, to miss the point completely. It is only the Spirit that gives us eyes to see and minds to comprehend what we read. He insisted that unless it is "inscribed by the finger and Spirit of God on the heart, it is but a dead letter, and as it were a lifeless thing."[10]

Orthodox Calvinism tended to lose the tension between Word and Spirit. The emphasis was put on the Word rationally understood, leaving little room for the movement of the Spirit. It became literal and dogmatic. Literalism has been a continuing tendency in the Reformed tradition and has frequently provided the primary method of interpretation of scripture. Even though the Westminster Assembly in the seventeenth century was the supreme achievement, some would say the triumph, of orthodox Calvinism, the Confession is nevertheless faithful to Calvin's delicate balance between Word and Spirit when it declares, "We acknowledge the inward illumination of the Spirit of God to be necessary for the saving understanding of such things as are revealed in the Word."[11]

Calvin set the model for a Reformed approach to scripture which can still be helpful to us. It is a considerable improvement over the commonly developed habits. It followed the following guidelines:

1. It pays close attention to the context of a passage. Calvin himself said, "There are many statements in Scripture the meaning of which depends upon their context."[12] So also Thomas Goodwin, a Puritan, declared, "The right

context of Scripture is half the interpretation."[13] This
means that wresting a passage from its context or isolating
proof texts is contrary to the Reformed method of reading
or studying the Bible. Calvin bluntly warned of this danger:
"When passages of Scripture are taken up at random, and
no attention is paid to the context, we need not wonder that
mistakes . . . frequently arise."[14] Many errors still arise
because people do not pay attention to this principle.

Whenever people cite particular verses of scripture to
support a point of view, one can usually conclude that what
is going on is proof-texting out of context. Scripture has its
own integrity and is to be respected. The biblical authors
carefully constructed their works, usually independently of
each other. Most efforts to take a verse from one writer to
support a verse from another book of scripture are likely to
misunderstand the meaning of the text by imposing an
outside meaning on it.

Reformed treatment of scripture pays attention to the
context, sees verses as part of a creative whole, and respects
the individuality of the authors.

2. It uses the scholarly tools available. Calvin knew the
biblical languages, was concerned about recovering the
original meaning of the authors, and sought out the natural
meaning of the text. He used the tools for biblical scholarship available to him at the time and was not afraid to be
critical of the text. He recognized that getting the meaning
of a text is a difficult task. God "speaks openly, and utters
nothing that is deceitful or ambiguous. But experience tells
us that Scripture is somewhat dark and hard to be understood."[15] Following Calvin's lead, the Reformed approach
to scripture has not hesitated to utilize the most rigorous
biblical scholarship.

Reformed biblical scholarship has assisted Christians by
providing helpful historical, sociological, and linguistic
perspectives. These have served to assist in the process of
making the bridge from the ancient culture in which the
texts were originally set to our contemporary culture.
Scholarship has often helped to make scripture relevant to

people who would otherwise see only its cultural strangeness or, by failure to respect cultural difference, rush to apply a passage from a different context to our own without any appreciation for the difficulty inherent in this.

3. The Bible has a fundamental unity, which includes both the Old and New Testaments. When we are perplexed by a particular New Testament passage, it is helpful to examine it and explain it by Old Testament passages that may shed light on it. Calvin insisted on this unity, and went so far as to say that the covenant in the Old Testament "is so much like ours in substance and reality that the two are actually one and the same."[16] Because Calvin understood that all revelation is of Christ the Mediator, he interpreted Old Testament passages in the light of the incarnation, while at the same time seeking to understand the intention of the authors who spoke to people in their own time.

As followers of Calvin, the Puritans took the Old Testament as seriously as the New, because they believed it was the same God revealed in both and the same revelation of God's will to be found in both. Reformed churches have continued this respect for the Old Testament. It is characteristic of the Reformed tradition to take the Old Testament seriously. John Knox insisted on the reading of an Old Testament and a New Testament lesson for every Sunday, and that pattern was continued by the Westminster divines in the first Directory for the Worship of God. The regular reading of the Old Testament is symbolic of the high regard Reformed Christians have paid to this part of the Bible.

4. Because reading scripture is not easy and its meaning is not obvious, we need the assistance of the Holy Spirit so that we may actually encounter the living word of God in our reading. This was the basis for Calvin's insistence on the central importance of the illumination of the Holy Spirit. "I grant that doctrines ought to be tested by God's word; but except the Spirit of wisdom be present, to have God's word in our hands will avail little or nothing, for its meaning will not appear to us."[17] Understanding the Bible is never simply a matter of mechanical reading, but in-

volves the reader in a process of prayerful and attentive work.

Our acknowledgment that the text is difficult may open us to new understanding. As we are stretched in our reading, seeking to discover what God has to say to us, we may see a passage in a completely new light. Our patience with the text may also produce an attitude of humility in us as readers. Admission that we do not have all the answers may be a requirement for genuine encounter with God's word.

5. Scripture must be understood in relationship to what it leads us to do. John White declared, "Practice and not bare knowledge is, or should be, the end and fruit of the study of the Scriptures."[18] He is consistent with the teaching of the Westminster Shorter Catechism with which this chapter begins. The Bible is not an abstract set of principles but a guide for the Christian life in community. The reading of scripture is toward an end, that of shaping and reforming the church so that believers may become more faithful and obedient in their life in the world.

The Second Helvetic Confession summarizes a classic Reformed approach to the study of scripture in these words:

> We hold that interpretation of the Scripture to be orthodox and genuine which is gleaned from the Scriptures themselves (from the nature of the language in which they were written, likewise according to the circumstances in which they were set down, and expounded in the light of like and unlike passages and of many and clearer passages) and which agree with the rule of faith and love, and contributes much to the glory of God and [human] salvation.[19]

Reformed Protestants encounter scripture in a variety of ways and forms. They are assisted by these encounters in the development of their spirituality. They cannot escape responsibility to be interpreters, because scripture is so much a part of the life of the Reformed. In a variety of ways, scripture is central to the experience of believers.

The Use of Scripture in Preaching and Teaching

The preaching of the Word has always been a principal means of grace for Reformed Christians. Preaching has been so central in the life of Reformed churches that it can be said to have a sacramental character. T.H.L. Parker, the great biographer of Calvin, clarifies this: "The sermon, we might say, is the audible Eucharist, the Lord's Supper the visible Eucharist. Calvin was fond of saying that in the pulpit Christ must preside. The verb is significant, reminding us of the 'president' of the Eucharist in the early Church."[20] Because Reformed Protestants have experienced the presence of God in the preaching of the Word, the moment when the preacher ascends the pulpit is frequently one of awe and hushed expectancy. The people are attentive because they are waiting to hear a word from the Lord. Even years of poor preaching do not seem to discourage Reformed Christians from their deeply held hope that they will hear a word from the Lord in the preaching.

Calvin made no absolute distinction between the Word read and the Word proclaimed. The sermon was just as much the Word of God as the scripture lesson. The words of the preacher were the Word of God to the extent that they were a faithful interpretation of the living Word, Jesus Christ. Both the writers of scripture and the preachers are human instruments used by the Holy Spirit. The preacher is an ambassador of God, and the only authority the preacher can have is the calling from God to preach and the faithfulness of the preacher to preach only what is commanded in Holy Scripture.

Calvin followed the practice of some of the early church theologians such as Augustine, John Chrysostom, and Ambrose of reading and preaching through books of the Bible in sequence. With other Reformers, particularly Zwingli, he broke with the medieval lectionary (a listing of brief texts for each Sunday of the year), because he believed that the scriptures needed to be proclaimed and interpreted in context. He believed that the lectionary severed the lesson from its larger context. He therefore preached on an

Old Testament text on weekdays and on the New Testament
on Sundays. Ordinarily, Calvin preached on a few verses at
a time, and this meant that he took a long time to complete
a single book of the Bible. He preached 123 sermons on
Genesis alone!

Calvin worked hard to present the message of the text
and then to apply it to the lives of the hearers. In his closing
words to the ministers of Geneva just before he died, he
said this about his preaching and teaching:

> As to my doctine, I have taught faithfully, and God has given
> me grace to write what I have written as faithfully as it was in
> my power. I have not falsified a single passage of the
> Scriptures, nor given it a wrong interpretation to the best of
> my knowledge; and though I might have introduced subtle
> senses, had I studied subtlety, I cast that temptation under
> my feet and always aimed at simplicity.[21]

Reformed preaching, especially in its formative period,
tended to follow Calvin's example. It usually avoided the
lectionary for the same reason that Calvin rejected it—
because it cut the Bible into separate and unrelated scraps,
which were presented arbitrarily and out of context. He
preached in sequence through an entire book of the Bible;
each sermon thus had the context of previous or following
sermons, and each book of the Bible was given attention
through a period of time. John Knox (the major leader of
the Reformation in Scotland) took that method of preaching with him to Scotland and began a tradition of great
exegetical preaching, which was solidly based on a text that
was understood in its context, carefully explained, and then
applied to the situation of the hearers.

Hearing the Word does not automatically result from
hearing the words of scripture read or proclaimed. The
members of the congregation have a responsibility to
participate in the preaching process. William Perkins, an
English Puritan, advised: "To the profitable hearing of
Gods Word three things are required: Preparation before
we hear, a right disposition in hearing, and duties to be

practiced afterward."[22] The congregation is anything but passive in the process. The people have a duty to work to understand the preacher, and they must, therefore, approach the matter of hearing the Word with anticipatory faith. It is also imperative that they approach the sermon with open minds ready to receive what is preached as a word from God. The Reformed practice of preceding the public and private reading of scripture with prayer for right hearing is the ritual act that points to this important understanding of the difference between the external, outward Word and the internal, living Word.

The Use of Scripture in Worship

Another means through which Reformed Christians have encountered the Bible is music. The hearty singing that has generally characterized Reformed worship contains frequent fragments of biblical passages, and even more frequent paraphrases of biblical material. To become familiar with Reformed hymnody is to learn to love the Bible by becoming familiar with its language and imagery.

The psalms have continued to have a special place in Reformed hymnody. Calvin sought to restore the use of the psalms in public worship. The development of a sung psalter for use by all the people was one of his primary achievements.

Two recently published American hymnals for Reformed denominations, *Rejoice in the Lord* for the Reformed Church in America and *The Presbyterian Hymnal: Hymns, Psalms, and Spiritual Songs* for the Presbyterian Church (U.S.A.), both contain long sections of the sung psalter. They illustrate a revival of interest in singing the psalms.

Calvin understood the psalms as prayers, so that when the psalms were sung the congregation was praying. Congregational singing was thus the principal liturgical work of the people.

Congregational singing became the focus of the activity of the people in Reformed churches. The hymnal was really the Reformed prayer book. It contained praises, confession, thanksgiving, and petition, all set to music. Edwards, writing in the midst of the Great Awakening, emphasized the importance of music: "The duty of singing praises to God, seems to be appointed wholly to excite and express religious affections. No other reason can be assigned, why we should express ourselves to God in verse, rather than in prose, and do it with music, but only, that such is our nature and frame, that these things have a tendency to move our affections."[23] We remember what we have sung much more easily than what we have spoken. Biblical phrases and expressions from our hymns are fixed in our memories because they are associated with melodies that we remember.

We use the psalms as reminders of the faith of the whole church and as a summary of our sacred history. We also use them to express what is most private and personal. They deal with us, with our deepest longings, our fears, our doubts, our anger, our delight. When we read the psalms, they become, in Calvin's words, "'an Anatomy of all the Parts of the Soul;' for there is not an emotion of which any one can be conscious that is not here represented as in a mirror."[24] They reflect and express back to us who we are and how we stand before God. There are few human emotions that the psalms do not express. They give us permission to accept our own feelings. If, for example, I am angry at God or have feelings of bitterness toward another person, I do not have to feel guilty for having those emotions; I can read in the psalms those same feelings and know that I do not have to pretend before God that I do not feel what I feel. The psalms give permission to claim our own experience.

In the act of hearing the Word read and proclaimed, the believer is confronted by the living Word. The possibility for spiritual renewal through the encounter with God in public worship is enhanced through the singing of hymns and psalms that use the words, phrases, and images of the Bible. This language helps to shape us; it becomes a part of us. When we most need the comfort or guidance of scripture, it is the language of hymns that is most likely to be accessible to us.

Private Reading and Study

In addition to the ways through which believers are enabled to encounter the Bible in the public forms of preaching, teaching, and public worship, the Reformed tradition has maintained a high place for the private reading of scripture. The public and corporate uses of scripture act as a corrective upon private reading, preventing it from becoming too introspective, but they do not replace it as a central feature of Reformed piety.

After hearing the Word preached, the devout Puritan was encouraged to meditate upon what had been heard. Lewis Bayly, in his manual for the Christian life, suggested, "As thou returnest home, or when thou art entered into thy House, meditate a little while upon those things, which thou hast heard. And as the clean beasts Which chew the cud; so must thou bring again to thy remembrance, that which thou hast heard in the Church."[25] Family conversation in Reformed homes on the Lord's Day included discussion of the sermon and of the way the preacher used the biblical text. The heads of households were instructed to have all members of the family repeat parts of the catechism and to account for what they had learned from the sermon. Thus, there was a direct carryover from public worship to family study and devotions.

Bayly and other Puritan divines strongly advised that every Christian individual or family read a full chapter of scripture at the beginning and ending of every day and at noon. Bayly said the whole Bible can thus be read through in a year, except for the last six chapters, which were to be read on the last day of the year.[26] This extensive reading, added to regular hearing of the preached Word, enabled these Reformed Protestants to become well acquainted with scripture. The language of the Bible was familiar to them, and they were able to use its images in their prayers.

Bible study has an important and highly valued place in

the pilgrimage of every individual Christian, and especially within the Reformed tradition. This study is aimed at the discovery of the meaning of a given passage by considering who the author was, to whom the passage was addressed, the social, political, and historical context in which it was written, and its central themes. Such study is hard work, yet it is necessary if we are to come to an understanding of the text. The Reformed churches have prized their scholars and insisted that their pastors have a scholarly introduction to scripture. Every congregation ought to be a place in which the Bible is read with care and attention to the scholarly tools that are available and used. Too often, pastors have not given the people credit for an ability to accept and grow from the insights of scholars, and otherwise intelligent Christians are left with childish attitudes toward the Bible. The classes that are offered frequently stop at the introductory level and fail to provide for those who are ready for more intense study.

Knowing the content of the Bible is not enough, however. Bayly suggested that after reading scripture, the Christian is to meditate about "how many excellent things thou canst remember out of it."[27] Knowledge does not lead to an automatic transformation of our lives. A serious limitation of much of the best Bible study is that it does not make the bridge to the lives of people. People have good information about the text without being confronted by what the text has to do with them.

Richard Baxter, seeking to preserve the best of Puritanism after the restoration of the monarchy, described the common Puritan practice of "consideration" as a means of opening "the door between the head and the heart. The understanding, having received truths, lays them up in the memory, and consideration conveys them from thence to the affections."[28] He makes the distinction between the "best scholar whose apprehension is quick, clear, and tenacious," and the "best Christian whose apprehension is the deepest and most affectionate and who has the readiest passages, not so much from the ear to the brain as from that to the heart."[29]

Baxter is advocating a way of approaching scripture that stands alongside the scholarly approach. It goes hand in hand with it, but is different. John Owen, Baxter's contemporary, depicted it as "meditating upon what respect and relevance there is between the Word and our own heart, so that they stay close together in conformity to each other."[30] Bayly speaks about this same method of reading when he advises, "Apply these things to thine own heart and read not these chapters, as matter of historical discourse: but as if they were so many letters or epistles sent down from God out of heaven unto thee."[31] Devotional reading of scripture is a personal approach to a particular passage, in which the goal is to see how it sheds light on our own particular situation or calls us to a new self-understanding.

Richard Baxter's practice of what he calls "consideration" of the text seeks to make the connection between the text and ourselves. He advises the practice of "soliloquy" or "preaching to one's self." Thus, every Christian must become a preacher to his/her own soul, using the same method that a preacher would use in a sermon. In the same way the preacher takes with the hearts of the people, so the individual Christian "take with thy own heart." He puts it in these clear terms: "Explain to thyself the things on which thou dost meditate; confirm thy faith in them from scripture; and then apply them to thyself, according to their nature and thy own necessity."[32]

This method of devotional reading of scripture was common among the Puritans. It owes a great deal to the Benedictine monastic method of *lectio divina,* which read the text, following a carefully devised process of prayer, reading, meditation, and contemplation of the text and its meaning. John White described the process in some detail, saying that the first responsibility is to discover the meaning of the words. Then the reader should choose those things from the text that may be most helpful and apply them directly. After that is done, "we must whet them upon our hearts, till they warme, and quicken our affections."[33]

Such reading is the act of approaching the Bible with openness to the mystery of God, who uses these ancient texts in order to speak a fresh word to us today. We are drawn to scripture because of the comfort and sense of God's presence that we discover there. At the same time, we stand in awe at the ethical demands of God's will which we also find there. The key is in our response to what we have read. As we read, we internalize a passage so that it becomes a *living word* for us.

Belief that God can be encountered through reading and meditation on the biblical text is an important part of our motivation for spending time with the Bible. Unless we discover that there is something more at stake than learning about ancient customs or historical events, something that has to do with our own lives, we shall quite likely leave the Bible to the experts. Our goal is to encounter in the writings out of the distant past, clothed in their own cultural baggage, a personal word from God. This cannot happen until we see ourselves addressed by the text and apply what we hear to our own lives. Dietrich Bonhoeffer, the twentieth-century German theologian and martyr, wrote, "Just as you do not analyse the words of someone you love, but accept them as they are said to you, accept the Word of Scripture and ponder it in your heart. . . . That is meditation."[34]

Devotional reading of scripture is the effort to be genuinely open to whatever God has for us in a passage. It requires that a person expect something from what is read, to be truly looking for a word from God. Calvin says that we must be "emptied of our own understanding" in order to have a "saving acquaintance with God."[35] This is not easy to do, because we are all accustomed to reading the Bible in order to learn something. To the extent that we read the Bible in order to reinforce our answer to an important question, we may be unable to learn what God is saying to us. We already *know* what we are looking for, or are already familiar with the passage and bring deeply held assumptions about the meaning, so that it is not really possible to be expectant of anything new.

Devotional reading of scripture takes time for reflection

while reading. We are not rewarded for reading a lot of material. Too often people make promises to read the whole Bible from cover to cover, and find it nearly impossible to achieve the goal. In their haste to cover too much material, they miss what is really there. Bayly, who instructed his readers to read a chapter every morning, noon, and evening, had this to say about the amount of scripture to be read: "One chapter thus read with understanding, and meditated on with application, will better feed and comfort thy soul, than five read and run over without marking their scope or sense, or making any use thereof to thine own self."[36] Our natural tendency is to want to read too much in order to have a sense of accomplishment. In our effort to push ahead with our reading, we are quite likely to miss what it has to say to us.

There are some basic steps to follow for responsible private reading of scripture if we are to be faithful to the text and fruitful in our search to be guided by the Word of God.

We need to approach the text with reverence and openness to what we may discover. We cannot escape the fact that we all bring our own issues, problems, concerns, and hurts to the text. Our goal in approaching scripture devotionally is to be led to new discoveries about ourselves in the light of God's word for us, and to be enabled to move from reading the text for information to being led by the text to a deeper relationship with God.

We need to approach the text prayerfully, trusting that God speaks through these ancient words and will speak to us in a personal way. John Bunyan, the Puritan martyr for religious liberty, was aware of both the difficulties and possibilities of reading scripture. "I have sometimes seen more in a line of the Bible, than I could well tell how to stand under; and yet at another time the whole Bible hath been to me as dry as a stick: or rather, my heart hath been so dead and dry unto it, that I could not conceive the least dram of refreshment though I have looked it all over."[37] That experience is true of all of us who have sought to discover God's presence and will in the Bible. Without an inner openness, we may find nothing at all. If, on the other hand, we can be ready to hear what God has to say, we may be surprised by a fresh and startling discovery.

One of the delights of the scriptures is that they can be fresh and new with each reading. To read them over and over is to discover that they do not wear out with rereading. They take on new meaning with each pondering over them. They both express and shape our piety. Richard Baxter advised his readers to deal with scripture by the exercise of their imaginations, using what he called "biblical images." In spite of his warning against looking at drawn pictures, which he feared might lead to idolatry, he suggested that they "get the liveliest picture of them [biblical characters, stories, and situations] that thou possibly canst by contemplating the scripture account of them."[38] The use of the imagination can serve as a focus for our attention while reading, and it can enable us to put ourselves into the text so that we discover ourselves as the ones being addressed in such a way that we are confronted with the need to respond.

This kind of discovery happens when we spend time with the Bible. We can all read the Bible in different translations and discover that we are refreshed and led to new meanings by the different ways of using words. Even more important, by spending reflective time with the Bible we can all have the doors opened to the power of the Holy Spirit, which can take the familiar words and make them words about ourselves. What we bring to the text will, of course, shape what we discover. If we are prepared to receive, we shall be nourished. We shall see that our faith, our life, our experience are reflected back to us in unexpected ways.

It may be helpful to follow an established procedure for reading and praying with the scriptures. There are certain steps in the process that have been used in many traditions of Christianity, including especially the Benedictines and the Puritans. The process can be helpful for us still. In the seventeenth century, George Webbe, an influential Puritan writer, suggested this process: "Before reading pray unto God to bless thee in that action. In reading, settle thyself to do it with attention. After reading, apply it to thyself, for thy instruction, in thy practice and imitation."[39]

The following suggestions for meditative reading of scripture may be followed by individuals or in small groups. There is a certain value to the group method if all members are truly encouraged to speak up and if there is no intimidation or subtle notion that the leader has the right answers. Whether alone or in company, the steps for praying the Bible are these:

First, we take time to collect ourselves before reading. We quiet ourselves and prepare to be receptive. We do this so that we bring as little of our previous assumptions as possible. John White, a Puritan who wrote extensively about the devotional use of scripture, advised that we must free ourselves "from all incumbrances that pester the heart," that we must "awe" our hearts with holy reverence, and that our souls "must be quickened with a spiritual appetite" and our "faith must be stirred up and strengthened to believe it."[40] We seek to be genuinely open to whatever God has for us. We come to the Bible in prayer and with an open spirit. It is a good practice, for example, to spend a few minutes in silence before actually reading the text.

Second, we read the passage slowly, spending time with the words and letting our minds wander creatively as various words and images suggest other parts of scripture or events in our own lives. There is no particular need to work at getting through a whole chapter—we may pause halfway through because we are caught by a particularly powerful image. We need to learn to focus on smaller amounts of scripture. Dietrich Bonhoeffer recommended spending a week with a single text of ten to fifteen verses.[41]

As we repeat the words over and over, our minds are channeled and shaped in the process. Repetition is a way of training our minds and becoming attentive. Our minds are otherwise filled with distractions. The discipline of repetition is of more value to us in our busy world than it was for people of earlier centuries, who lived at a much slower pace. This is the value of memorization of scripture. In order to memorize a passage, it is necessary to repeat it over and over. We may discover that the familiarity thus bred is one that changes our behavior.

Third, we reflect on the passage and allow our mind to wander, making associations with our own experience, letting the questions come in new ways. A single word may be all that we need to dwell on at length. Side musings may be ways in which the Spirit is leading us to examine something that needs to be seen in the light of God's word for us. We may, for example, be reminded of other times when we have heard this particular passage and have been touched by God through this passage. The importance of keeping a journal handy cannot be exaggerated. It is an excellent way of keeping a record of impressions and associations. No matter how familiar we are with a particular passage, when we are open to a fresh hearing we discover that insight comes to us that we had not seen before. At times, the most familiar passage comes alive for us, and we discover something in the text we had not seen before.

Fourth, we meditate on the text so that we apply it to our own situation. This is the prayerful approach in which we really expect God to speak to us and are ready to hear. John White directs the reader, "After we have read any part of Scripture, our special care must be, when we have done, to recount and revolve in our mindes those things that we have read, and to meditate on them seriously."[42] We may not actually want to hear what God has to say to us, and we may resist the demands that seem to be made but we will not come away empty.

Fifth, we pray about the passage, allowing our praying to be shaped by what we have discovered, any new insights we have found. We will pray in gratitude for what we have found, with new power because we have seen ourselves there; we will offer our petitions, knowing what we need with new clarity. As we become opened to new discoveries about ourselves, we will also be enabled to pray for others with greater appreciation for their needs. Our prayers will spring from our study, and whether that praying takes place alone or in the company of others it will be prayer that has been deepened, corrected, and challenged. John White observed that although "Prayer and Reading of the Word be two distinct exercises, yet that they mutually help one another, is most manifest, and consequently are fit to be joyned together."[43] Prayer that follows reflection on scripture is what we mean by praying the Bible.

The prayer that Calvin frequently prayed before beginning his lectures is, itself, a model of what it means to bring the mind, upheld by the Holy Spirit, to the subject of scripture:

> May the Lord grant that we may engage in contemplating the mysteries of his heavenly wisdom with really increasing devotion, to his glory and to our edification. Amen.[44]

NOTES

1. Presbyterian Church (U.S.A.), *The Book of Confessions* (New York and Atlanta: Office of the General Assembly, 1983), 7.090.

2. *Book of Confessions,* 4.095.

3. Lewis Bayly, *The Practice of Piety* (London: Printed for Daniel Midwinter, at the Three Crowns in St. Paul's Churchyard, 1714), p. 101.

4. John Calvin, *Institutes of the Christian Religion,* ed. John T. McNeill, trans. Ford Lewis Battles (Philadelphia: Westminster Press, 1960), IV, VIII, 11, p. 1160.

5. Walter Wink, *The Bible in Human Transformation: Towards a New Paradigm for Biblical Study* (Fortress Press, Philadelphia: 1973), p. 77.

6. John Calvin, *Commentary on the Epistles of Paul the Apostle to the Corinthians,* trans. John Pringle (Grand Rapids: Wm. B. Eerdmans Publishing Co., 1948), 2 Cor. 3:6, p. 175.

7. John Calvin, *Commentaries on the Epistles of Paul to the Galatians and Ephesians,* 4:22, p. 135.

8. Calvin, *Institutes,* I, XIII, 1, p. 121.

9. Jack Rogers and Donald K. McKim, *The Authority and Interpretation of the Bible* (San Francisco: Harper & Row, 1979), p. 106.

10. John Calvin, *Commentaries on the Catholic Epistles,* trans.

and ed. John Owen (Grand Rapids: Baker Book House, 1984),
James 1:25, p. 297.
    11. Westminster Confession of Faith, *The Book of Confessions,*
6.006.
    12. Calvin, *Institutes,* IV, XVI, 23, p. 1346.
    13. Thomas Goodwin, *The Collected Works* (Edinburgh: James
Nichol & Co., 1861), vol. 5, p. 349.
    14. John Calvin, *Commentary on the Book of the Prophet Isaiah,*
trans. William Pringle (Grand Rapids: Baker Book House, 1984),
14:12, vol. 1, p. 442.
    15. John Calvin, *Commentary on Isaiah,* 45:19, vol. 2, p. 421.
    16. Calvin, *Institutes,* II, X, 2, p. 429.
    17. Calvin, *Commentaries on the Catholic Epistles,* 1 John 4:1,
p. 230.
    18. John White, *A Way to the Tree of Life: Discourses in Sundry
Directions for the Profitable Reading of the Scriptures* (London:
published by M.F. for R. Royston, 1647), p. 150.
    19. *Book of Confessions,* 5.010.
    20. T. H. L. Parker, *John Calvin: A Biography* (Philadelphia:
Westminster Press, 1975), p. 95.
    21. John Calvin, *Letters,* trans. M. R. Gilchrist, vol. IV, pp.
373–7.
    22. William Perkins, cited by Charles Hambrick-Stowe in *The
Practice of Piety: Puritan Devotional Disciplines in Seventeenth-
Century New England* (Chapel Hill, N.C.: University of North
Carolina Press, 1982), p. 110.
    23. Jonathan Edwards, *Religions Affections,* ed. John E. Smith,
The Works of Jonathan Edwards (New Haven: Yale University
Press, 1959), vol. 2, p. 115.
    24. John Calvin, *Commentaries: The Book of Psalms,* trans.
James Anderson (Grand Rapids: Baker Book House, 1984),
Preface, p. xxxvii.
    25. Bayly, *Practice of Piety,* p. 271.
    26. Bayly, *Practice of Piety,* pp. 141–42.
    27. Bayly, *Practice of Piety,* p. 140.
    28. Richard Baxter, *The Saints' Everlasting Rest* (New York:
Doubleday & Co., 1978), p. 143.
    29. Baxter, *Saints' Everlasting Rest,* p. 143.
    30. John Owen, *Sin and Temptation,* abr. and ed. James M.
Houston (Portland, Ore.: Multnomah Press, 1983), p. 44.
    31. Bayly, *Practice of Piety,* p. 140.
    32. Baxter, *Saints' Everlasting Rest,* p. 156.

33. White, *Way to the Tree of Life,* p. 151.

34. Dietrich Bonhoeffer, *The Way to Freedom,* ed. Edwin H. Robertson, trans. Edwin H. Robertson and John Bowden (London: Collins, 1966), p. 59.

35. Calvin, *Commentary: Corinthians,* 1 Cor 1:21, p. 84.

36. Bayly, *Practice of Piety,* p. 141.

37. John Bunyan, *Grace Abounding to the Chief of Sinners,* ed. Glenn Hinson (New York: Doubleday & Co., 1978), p. 306.

38. Baxter, *Saints' Everlasting Rest,* p. 159.

39. George Webbe, William Perkins, and Richard Rogers, *A Garden of Spiritual Flowers* (London: Robert Bird, 1635), p. 77.

40. White, *Way to the Tree of Life,* p. 137.

41. Bonhoeffer, *Way to Freedom,* p. 59.

42. White, *Way to the Tree of Life,* p. 150.

43. White, *Way to the Tree of Life,* p. 127.

44. John Calvin, *Devotions and Prayers of John Calvin,* ed. Charles E. Edwards (Grand Rapids: Baker Book House, 1954), p. 13.

5

Consultation:
Spiritual Guidance
in the Reformed Tradition

But we believe that this sincere confession which is made to God alone, either privately between God and the sinner, or publicly in the Church where the general confession of sins is said, is sufficient, and that in order to obtain forgiveness of sins it is not necessary for anyone to confess his sins to a priest, murmuring them in his ears, that in turn he might receive absolution from the priest with his laying on of hands. . . . If, however, anyone is overwhelmed by the burden of his sins and by perplexing temptations, and will seek counsel, instruction and comfort privately, either from a minister of the Church, or from any other brother [sic] who is instructed in God's law, we do not disapprove.

The Second Helvetic Confession[1]

One cannot be a Christian by oneself, in isolation from other people. The Christian faith is nurtured and expressed in relationships and must be experienced and lived out in some kind of community. This basic conviction about the corporate nature of the faith is emphasized in the Reformed tradition and appears in many places in the confessions. It is expressed in its most rigorous form as the insistence on the necessity of the church for salvation in the Second Helvetic Confession, which declares, "We deny that those can live before God who do not stand in fellowship with the true Church of God, but separate themselves from it. For as there was no salvation outside Noah's ark when the world perished in the flood; so we believe that there is no certain salvation outside Christ, who offers himself to be enjoyed by the elect in the Church."[2] This confessional position is not widely popular today. Even active church members seem to prefer to believe that the church is an extra added on to their basic private faith, which comes first. Reformed spirituality runs counter to the spirit of our time. It insists that the human spirit must be nurtured and directed by the community of faith.

In an age of individualism, this reminder of our need for one another is a healthy corrective. It serves to emphasize for us that the Christian's life cannot be lived without the guidance, support, and challenge of others. By ourselves, it is all too easy for us to mistake our own desires for signs of God's will. We interpret our experience in ways that serve our own purposes and hardly know that we are doing it. Thus we need the church, the companionship of other Christians, and personal relationships in which we can be mutually accountable and receive guidance from one another.

There have been several ways in which communal support and corrective guidance for individuals have been implemented in the history of the Christian church. They have been the primary ways in which the church has ministered to persons. The major forms have been: church discipline, confession, pastoral counseling, and spiritual guidance in the forms of individual personal care, correspondence, and informal mutual support. Sometimes the emphasis has been on one of these forms, sometimes on another, but all of them are directed toward the same goal, that of assisting Christians in the difficult task of remaining faithful and true to themselves.

Church Discipline

The first form of guidance began during the time of the development of the New Testament. The practice of re-

stricting someone from regular participation in the life of
the church and then of later lifting that restriction after a
time of penitence was identified as "binding and loosing."
Matthew's Gospel shows Jesus teaching the disciples to put
out those who will not listen to correction from an individual, or from a group of two or three, or finally from the
whole church (Matt. 18:15–18). This passage gives us a
picture of the method of church discipline in at least one
part of the first-century church. Church discipline was one
way in which individuals were brought to repentance and
change of life. Its purpose was not only maintaining the
purity of the whole church, but also providing pastoral
assistance to those who had committed scandalous acts. Its
goal was the reconciliation and healing of the persons
involved, not their punishment.

The practice of discipline in the church was revived by
Calvin after a period during which it had nearly disap-
peared. It was a way that Calvin exercised pastoral care.
The primary purpose of discipline is spiritual, not legal; it
accompanies the proclamation of the Word. Although
discipline could be arbitrary and cruel, and was often
self-righteous, it was also, at its best, a way of attending to
every member of the community. It took people seriously
enough to point out problems, warn of dangers, and call
them to accountability for their actions.

Because we live in an age in which tolerance has become a
primary virtue, we tend to view any effort at church
discipline as dangerously judgmental or interfering. Yet we
may also need to consider that our high value for tolerance
may be a way of avoiding expressions of genuine concern
for one another. If we do not care enough to pay attention
to one another's faults and then have the courage to deal
with them, we may be unwittingly admitting that our view
of the church is a group of lone individuals who gather
together as long as it pleases them and then go their way
alone, receiving no direct or honest support from the
community.

We are often guilty of quietly encouraging evil by refusing

to call others to account for their behavior. By our silence, and our fear of offending them, we neglect to care for them. Calvin warned about the dangers of this failure to challenge people who are in trouble. He was also concerned about the danger of being overly harsh. He suggested to those who were engaged in the exercise of discipline that it would be better "to season their admonitions with moderation."[3] He was concerned that excessive severity might discourage the weak and drive them farther from Christ.[4] The rigorous form of discipline that took place in Geneva during Calvin's tenure was for the purpose of repentance rather than punishment, and it was not intended to be undertaken without remorse and self-examination on the part of those passing judgment.

Reformed church discipline has traditionally sought to be faithful to scripture by requiring that private consultation take place as a first step. This private meeting with a pastor, elder, or other Christian for guidance, or with another pastor in cases of ministerial discipline, has been a means through which Reformed Christians have been kept from their own self-destructive devices.

It was only when private counsel was not heeded or when the person refused to accept the offer of such counsel that the next step in the process of discipline was used—appearance before the church session. Although the intention was still to protect the individual from disgrace except as a means of bringing about repentance, this was very difficult. Once discipline became a public matter, many abuses accompanied its exercise. It could be harsh, judgmental, and a forum for private vengeance. Persons could be used in the process to enhance the power of others. In spite of these and other abuses, and the overly rigorous means that this disciplinary process sometimes took, it was a way by which the Reformed churches accepted corporate responsibility for each member. They attempted to care for people caught in the web of sin and sought to bring to them the resources of forgiveness and new life.

Confession

The early church practiced public confession in the context of the gathered community. This public confession was an acknowledgment that Christians continued to need forgiveness, even though they had been redeemed by Christ. By the third century the practice of reconciliation of known sinners began to take more definite shape. Those who wanted to rejoin the community were to go to the bishop and confess their sin. They were required to perform some acts that demonstrated their seriousness and symbolized their sorrow for sin. Such acts of penitence included fasting, prayer, and giving alms to the poor. The rigor of this method of public discipline as a form of penitence gradually declined after the legalization of Christianity.

Private confession was a way by which the church sought to assist people with their own personal guilt and was an expression of pastoral care. Individuals were required to go to a priest for private confession before receiving Communion. Although private confession began as a voluntary practice, by 1214 it was declared to be a sacrament, and was required at least once a year. Perfect contrition, caused by the grace of God, was needed for the sins to be fully forgiven. The pastoral and personal problem was that people could never tell whether their contrition was perfect enough to merit forgiveness.

A more legalistic understanding developed in the late Middle Ages, which emphasized the words of absolution by the priest as the one thing needed for obtaining forgiveness. This was an effort to respond to the anxiety of many people about whether their contrition was complete enough. The confession, contrition, and assigned penance (prayers, fasting, or good deeds) were required for the sacrament to be helpful, but they were not essential for its validity.

Both Luther and Calvin somewhat reluctantly attacked the sacrament of penance, and both grounded their attack on their pastoral concern for people. Calvin saw that it was impossible to recount one's sins fully, "for experience convinces each one that, when we have at evening to examine the transgressions of only a single day, the memory is confused."[5] Thus he considered that the practice of required confession produced more evil than good, for it "can only destroy, condemn, confound, and cast into ruin and despair."[6] It led either to the practice of treating confession too lightly, and making superficial confession, or to a sense of hopelessness. He insisted that forgiveness cannot be tied to the practice of remembering one's sins and declaring them to a priest. Even when the minister is performing the office with humility and the recognition of limits, "the certainty of binding and loosing does not lie within the competence of earthly judgment because the minister of the word . . . can absolve only conditionally."[7] No one but God can know the state of the person's mind and heart, and it is God who forgives. For this reason he believed that all confession should be made to God, in either public or private prayer.

Calvin restored to corporate worship the ancient practice of the public prayer of confession. He made this corporate prayer normative for every service of public worship. The prayer of common confession became a standard feature of Reformed worship and the assurance of pardon a major source of spiritual consolation for Reformed Christians. Calvin says that when the whole church confesses itself guilty, "it is no common or light solace to have present there the ambassador of Christ, armed with the mandate of reconciliation, by whom it hears proclaimed its absolution."[8] In recent years, the assurance or pardon or declaration of absolution has lost some of its power. Pastors do not always realize how central this act is to the spiritual life of the people. Fear of clericalism is the usual excuse, but in the absence of a pastor forcefully declaring forgiveness, without ambiguity, the people are left with an uneasy feeling of guilt.

The second form of confession open to all Christians is private prayer. By themselves, people are free to unburden themselves of their personal guilt and to know that they receive the mercy of God, promised in Christ Jesus. In

private prayer, people can name sins they would be unable
to admit in a public setting. Public prayers of confession
must, of necessity, be general and inclusive. By its very
nature, private confession can be more deeply personal and
specific than any other form. The solitary individual need
not hesitate to confess any failing for fear of losing a
friendship or becoming less acceptable in the eyes of
another person. All that is required is that the person
believe wholeheartedly in the mercy and forgiveness of
God. Yet, that is a great deal to believe. Many people harbor
deep-seated ideas of a vengeful, unforgiving God, who
keeps score. They are thus unable to express fully their real
sense of sin, even though they know they cannot hide it
from God.

There are times when private confession is not enough,
when we need to tell another human being what we have
done and to have that person reassure us that we are
forgiven. The third form of confession is therefore that of
confessing our sins to another: "disclosing our weaknesses
to one another, we help one another with mutual counsel
and consolation."[9] This form of confession to another
person is not limited to pastors.

Like Luther, Calvin urged people to go to their pastors
for spiritual relief and solace. At the same time, he maintained that such confession must be "free so as not to be
required of all, but to be commended only to those who
know that they have need of it."[10] Confession to the pastor
was always a voluntary form of pastoral care within the
Reformed tradition. Confession could also be made to an
elder, or to any other church member.

Thus, although Calvin joined Luther in rejecting the
sacrament of penance, he certainly did not mean to cut off
Christians from the spiritual benefits of unburdening their
souls to a pastor or other Christian. "For it often happens
that one who hears general promises that are intended for
the whole congregation of believers remains nonetheless in
some doubt, and . . . still has a troubled mind."[11] Because
the practice was completely voluntary, the individual was
the only judge as to the content of what was revealed and

also had complete freedom of choice about the person to serve as the confessor.

One setting for confession to a pastor persisted long after the practice had generally fallen into disuse. On the Sunday before the Lord's Supper was celebrated, Calvin would announce that those who wished to receive Communion were required to inform him of their desire and arrange for a time for consultation, especially if they were not known to him or were under some suspicion about their manner of life. He explained that there were three reasons for this practice: First, it was to instruct believers more carefully in the faith; second, it was to assist those in need of correction; and third, it was to comfort any who were troubled by guilt. Although Calvin was careful to explain that he was not reintroducing required confession, he said that "he would prefer that system [required confession] to remain in force rather than to have no discipline at all."[12] Visiting with the pastor or an elder before coming to the sacrament of Communion remained a Reformed spiritual practice for many years, and is still a source of solace and healing for Reformed Christians in some parts of the world.

The principal purpose of making confession to a pastor was to provide help for people in dealing with their guilt, facing their sin, and accepting the grace and forgiveness of Christ. Calvin did not hesitate to pronounce words of absolution when people had confessed their sin. Reformed pastors have, however, been somewhat reluctant to follow his example. Many pastors have been very wary of anything that might suggest that they have any particular status as mediators between God and the people. Yet a great many people desperately need a clear and direct form of forgiveness. They are wallowing in guilt, and general statements are not sufficient to satisfy their need. Some people may need another person to say "You are forgiven" without any hesitation or reservation in order to be able to receive that good news.

In his novel *The Final Beast,* Frederick Buechner tells of a situation in which such a direct expression of forgiveness was necessary. In the scene Lillian Flagg, a deeply spiritual woman, is urging Nicolet, the pastor, to proclaim forgiveness to Rooney, a deeply disturbed woman. He argues that she already knows that he (the pastor) has forgiven her, but Lillian replies:

"She doesn't know God forgives her. That's the only power you have—to tell her that. Not just that he [God] forgives her the poor little adultery. But the faces she can't bear to look at now. . . . Tell her he [God] forgives her for being lonely and bored, for not being full of joy with a houseful of children. . . . Tell her that sin is forgiven because whether she knows it or not, that's what she wants more than anything else—what all of us want. What on earth do you think you were ordained for?"[13]

Now that mandatory confession has been relaxed as a rule in the Roman Catholic Church, Protestants may be able also to relax their fear of this practice. Pastors could indicate to parishioners that they are available for services of reconciliation. The results are likely to be surprising. The new Presbyterian volume *Services for Occasions of Pastoral Care,* a Supplemental Liturgical Resource, and the *Book of Worship* of the United Church of Christ both include orders for the reconciliation of the penitent, privately and communally.

Another form of self-examination, closely related to confession, developed by the Puritans was that of keeping diaries with such careful discipline that these journals have been called the Puritan confessional. The journals that survive show that these Puritans practiced rigorous self-examination as they wrote about events in their inner and outer lives. They also recorded special occasions when they experienced God's presence and power. Remembering these occasions enabled them to have courage in difficult moments and to gain a larger picture of God's plan for them, which renewed and strengthened faith. Although some of these journals still survive, it is true that many journal writers, especially women, left orders for them to be destroyed after their death.

An excellent example of a journal that survived is that of

Elizabeth White, who died in 1669 during childbirth. Her journal was widely printed in Boston, Glasgow, and London. It shows the way in which self-examination, combined with efforts to get help from others, finally led to a sense of secure faith. She begins by telling how she was in bondage to sin in spite of her father's efforts to bring her up as a Christian. It appears that her mother had been dead for some time, since she does not mention her. It is only as she approaches her marriage that she begins to develop a spiritual awareness: "I remember about a month before I was married, my Father would have me receive the Sacrament of the Lord's Supper, and I was very willing to it; until I considered what was required of those which did partake thereof."[14] She goes through the motions of obeying her father by visiting the pastor in what appears to be a kind of examination. Although she satisfies him, she knows that she has only pretended, and suddenly, soon after, she declares that the Lord "broke my false confidence, and swept away my refuge of lies."[15]

This dramatic experience took place during a sermon. She describes the event: "The Lord was pleased to open my heart as he did the heart of Lydia, so that I attended to the things that were spoken, and I perceived that my heart was not right in the sight of God."[16] The minister again came to see her and, although she was ashamed to tell him of her real spiritual condition, she felt the truth being forced from her. It is obvious that the pastor was a kind of spiritual director for her, and it further suggests that pastors' visits were anything but routine in those days.

While she was reading her Bible, some words of scripture became a significant turning point for her. "These words did support me very much, therefore, I wrote them out and laid them in my closet, that they might still be in my eye, that I might when I looked upon them be encouraged to hope in, and wait upon the Lord."[17] She was comforted by hearing "that a hypocrite seldom or never doubted his condition, and that it was a sign of sincerity, to desire a sincere heart."[18] A woman friend came to visit and she related her condition but her relief was only temporary.

For a long period she was alone with her doubts about herself and anxious about her possible death as she faced childbirth. It was during the time of delivery of her child that she was comforted by scripture. She survived one childbirth and a postpartum depression, which she described as a struggle with Satan, but she faced another crisis connected to the weaning of her baby.

> And since my child was weaned, I was in such a state of deadness and darkness, that I thought if I was ever raised out of it, I should never question my condition again; I was tempted to think that the Scripture was not the Word of God? I had let out my affection in a wonderful measure to my child, and yet my Lord forsook me not, but dispelled my darkness, and filled me with rejoicing: O what shall I render to him?[19]

Elizabeth White's story shows how a woman was able to make the connection between the spiritual growth or change in her life and the events of marriage, pregnancy, childbirth, and weaning her baby. She uses her experiences as a woman to provide images for her spiritual journey, from her father's control and protection to her relative independence as a married woman, and from her fear of death to confidence in herself as a child of God. She also sees her experience of weaning her child as a symbol of her own weaning from dependence on secondhand faith to a genuine experience of the personal grace of God.

Her journal illustrates the practice of confessing, for help, to a pastor and also to another woman friend. Her diary is an excellent example of the way Puritans used their journals to reflect on their own experiences. These journals were a disciplined form of confession and of spiritual self-direction.

All three forms of confession—corporate public prayer, private prayer including self-examination and journal writing, and spoken confession to another person—are expressions of the power of the keys that Calvin understood to be the power of the Word of God proclaimed. Ministers exercise the power of the keys when they proclaim the gospel, and they do this in preaching, teaching, and private counsel.

Pastoral Counseling

A significant part of the work of the pastor has always been counseling the members of the congregation and other people who seek such guidance and nurture. Pastoral counseling is the expression of the accepting love of God by persons, ordained or not, who act on behalf of the church to assist people in their efforts to deal with inner conflicts, unresolved problems, questions about the meaning of life, difficulties in relationships, and other matters that perplex them. The counselor seeks to assist the person to come to terms with the problem, resolve the conflict, or find healing for the wound.

Pastoral counseling has taken many different forms in different cultural settings and periods of history. At times it has focused almost exclusively on the work of the ordained; at other times it has been shared by many members of the community of faith. Although she confesses that she did not properly receive the gifts offered to her, Elizabeth White was visited by both her pastor and a woman friend, and something like pastoral counseling took place. Within the Reformed tradition, the office of elder was well suited for providing pastoral care and helped to multiply the human resources available to the people.

Counseling can take its shape from reflection on the nature of the gospel message, or it can be strongly influenced, even dominated, by the human science of psychology, or, more likely, it can be a blend of the two disciplines. Counseling preceded modern psychology, however. Richard Baxter's efforts to restore dignity and motivation to a dispirited Puritan clergy, following the Restoration and the seeming defeat of the Puritan dream, were evidence of how important counseling was in the seventeenth century. It was composed of common sense, biblical maxims, love, and carefully developed ways of responding to particular situations that were the inheritance of medieval Roman Catholic pastoral manuals.

Above all, Baxter insisted that pastors make themselves available to the members of the congregation, because every single member ought to have personal recourse to the pastor "for resolving of their doubts, and for help against their sins, and for direction in duty, and for increase of knowledge and all saving grace."[20] These four needs suggest the basis for Puritan pastoral counseling. It consisted of counseling people with problems, pronouncing forgiveness for those who were trapped in guilt, giving guidance for those confused about the direction of their lives, and teaching the faith.

By modern standards, most of this counseling was very directive. It consisted of biblical injunctions, and seems severe and demanding. Cotton Mather describes his parental counseling with his daughter, Katy. He says that he warned her of his coming death and then pointed out her sinful condition. "I gave her to understand, that when I am taken from her, she must look to meet with more humbling afflictions than she does, now she has a careful and a tender father to provide for her; but, if she would pray constantly, God in the Lord Jesus Christ, would be a Father to her, and make all afflictions work together for her good."[21] The modern reader almost instinctively shrinks back from this account, feeling sorry for the child, wondering at the insensitivity of the father who appears to frighten her deliberately. Yet Mather was expressing his love for his child and his parental concern for her well-being. He was doing the best he could to provide pastoral counseling. His was typical of the pastoral counseling that prevailed until quite recently.

In spite of our twentieth-century eagerness to criticize everything prior to our time as uninformed, insensitive, or cruel and self-righteous, we need to look upon the methods of pastoral counseling that existed prior to modern science with a willingness to appreciate that they accomplished much of what they set out to do. They assisted great numbers of people in dealing with the tragedies of life. They provided guidance for people who were perplexed. They offered hope to people caught in despair and depression. They were expressions of the love of the gospel.

Only after the 1930s, when an experimental program was developed at Massachusetts General Hospital for training pastors, did modern pastoral counseling enter into the curriculum of theological seminary education. Giants such as Anton Boisen, Seward Hiltner, Carl Rogers, and Wayne Oates were the pioneers in the effort to apply the insights of the new science of psychology to pastoral care. In so doing, they brought enormous contributions to the field of pastoral counseling. They helped to provide a basis for an approach to people's problems that allowed for more listening and was less eager to supply solutions. They enabled pastors to avoid judgment and to seek to understand the complexities of the lives laid open before them. They humanized the practice of pastoral counseling.

Yet at the same time it must also be said that they helped to lead counseling away from explicit connection to Christian symbols and language. The psychological dimension of counseling sometimes controlled the method almost to the exclusion of the religious. It was often difficult to tell a secular counselor apart from a religious one. The specialization of pastoral counseling also centered the work in the person of the pastor, removing other church members from participation in it because they were not "properly" trained. A result of this trend has been that many pastors spend most of their time counseling troubled people, almost to the exclusion of other activities.

People have sensed that there is something missing in psychological pastoral counseling. They have sought for mature Christians who might assist them in their spiritual struggles, help them to sort out their religious experiences, deal with their efforts to improve their prayers, and guide them in discerning God's will for them. Pastors have not been trained for responding to this need, and may be somewhat awkward in the presence of the kinds of questions that are asked of them. Thus the ancient practice of spiritual direction/guidance has new relevance for Protestant pastors and people today.

Spiritual Guidance

The practice of spiritual consultation or direction has a long history. We might say that it began with the work of Paul, who established close relationships with converts, even comparing himself to a human father to them: "For though you might have ten thousand guardians in Christ, you do not have many fathers. . . . I became your father through the gospel" (1 Cor. 4:15). With particular individuals such as Timothy and with whole congregations, he gave advice, admonished, and even urged others to imitate him as he imitated Christ.

As early as the third century the practice of revealing the condition of one's soul to a spiritual "guide" or "director" became common. Many Christians went out to the desert hermits during the fourth century for such guidance, and the practice spread widely. The "director" would give advice about prayer and would suggest appropriate works of repentance. Many of the great "spiritual directors" of the ages have been women, quite often members of monastic orders rather than ordinary laypeople. These women exercised tremendous influence on their times and were sought after as personal guides by rich and powerful women and men.

Among Protestants, the practice of regularly turning to a guide for assistance with one's spiritual life has been less common than among Roman Catholics. This was, in part, because of the central importance of private prayer and private reading of scripture, which tended to make people value their personal relationship with God more than their need for one another. Spiritual guidance became an option which many Reformed Protestants did not understand or appreciate.

Among the Puritans, however, the practice of seeking spiritual guidance from one's neighbor or pastor was revived. Perhaps because they practiced their faith with such earnestness, they discovered that they could not function by their own light alone. Francis Rous suggested that when a person is experiencing a time of dryness and feels abandoned by Christ, when "she can hardly see by her own light, another that hath light for the time, (though perchance clouded himself as much or more another time) may tell her what he sees by his light. And indeed when the soul is in the dark, and her own light shines not, she may do well to get a guide, and to take heed to borrowed light, until the day dawn and the day-star arise in her own heart."[22] Since Puritanism was a grass-roots movement of the people, pastors were not the center of spiritual guidance. People tended to choose their peers. This was especially true of women, who became spiritual guides for one another.

Letter-Writing

At the time of the Reformation, Protestants picked up a common form of spiritual direction, letter-writing, and made it their own. This was necessitated, in part, because of the inability of many people to find a pastor or guide close by. In their geographic isolation, they were forced to use letters to get the help they needed.

Calvin exercised much of his pastoral care by writing letters. The letters show his method of spiritual guidance. An excellent example of this guidance is in his letters to Madame de Cany: "But seeing that it is his [God's] pleasure that we should be separated by so great a distance, which does not permit more frequent communication between us, I beseech you, Madame, to take what I do write as a testimony of the earnest desire which I have to promote your salvation."[23] This letter not only shows Calvin's pastoral concern, but indicates clearly why he chose the method of correspondence to provide guidance for her.

Calvin also used letters as a means of finding spiritual guidance for himself from William Farel and Martin Bucer. He poured out his own griefs and problems to Farel: "The death of Courault has so overwhelmed me, that I can set no bounds to my grief. . . . It is not merely the want of sleep, to which custom has so inured me, by which I am harassed, but I am utterly exhausted by these melancholy thoughts all night long."[24] He regretted the lack of opportunity to confide in Farel personally and thus seek his help and advice. On the occasion of the death of his wife, he revealed a side of himself rarely noticed by historians. He wrote, "I subdue my grief as well as I can. Friends, also, are earnest in their duty to me. It might be wished, indeed, that they could profit me and themselves more; yet one can scarcely say how much I am supported by their attentions. But you know well enough how tender, or rather soft, my mind is."[25]

In spite of his heavy preaching, teaching, and administrative responsibilities, Calvin believed it was important to exercise this pastoral care for individuals in crisis. He was at least as much a pastor and director of souls as he was scholar, administrator, and theologian. We can only be amazed that he found time for all these activities in his schedule.

Samuel Rutherford, the Scottish Presbyterian, also wrote letters of spiritual counsel, in which he was sometimes quite direct in his advice, and nowhere more so than when dealing with doubt. He wrote, "I desire your sister, in her fears and doubtings, to fasten her grips on Christ's love. I forbid her to doubt; for Christ loveth her, and hath her name written in His book."[26]

Perhaps Rutherford's clearest advice took the form of an outline of a method of prayer and Christian conduct, which he had been requested to provide even though he recognized that he, himself came short:

> 1. That hours of the day, less or more time, for the word and prayer, be given to God. . . .
> 2. In the midst of worldly employments, there should be some thoughts of sin, death, judgment, and eternity, with at least a word or two of ejaculatory prayer to God.
> 3. To beware of wandering of heart in private prayers.
> 4. Not to grudge, howbeit ye come from prayer without a sense of joy. . . .

5. That the Lord's-day, from morning to night, be spent always either in private or public worship.

6. That words be observed, wandering and idle thoughts be avoided, sudden anger and desire of revenge, even of such as persecute the truth, be guarded against; for we often mix our zeal with our wild-fire.

7. That known, discovered, and revealed sins, that are against the conscience, be eschewed, as most dangerous preparatives to hardness of heart.

8. That in dealing with men, faith and truth in covenants and trafficking be regarded."[27]

Mutuality in Guidance

The Protestant Reformation did not completely eliminate the role of the nonordained spiritual guide. People continued to seek out friends who were not ordained in order to unburden themselves. Calvin stressed the need for mutuality: "We should lay our infirmities on one another's breasts, to receive among ourselves spiritual counsel, mutual compassion, and mutual consolation."[28] This mutuality did not require the presence of any ordained person.

The black church took this mutual exercise of the ministry of spiritual guidance seriously. One example of this ministry of the laity is reported by Howard Thurman: "Once you had joined the church, the next step in your validation was to be placed under the tutelage of older members. Often there were two, a man and a woman, who were spiritual guides assigned to you."[29] He describes an incident in his life in which his sponsor was direct in reprimanding him, and concludes: "Looking back, it is clear to me that the watchful attention of my sponsors in the church served to enhance my consciousness that whatever I did with my life mattered. They added to the security given to me by the quiet insistence of my mother and especially my grandmother that their children's lives were a precious gift."[30]

The black church was a kind of extended family, which

could withstand the hostility of the white world and provide support, training, and education for its own members by utilizing the skills and faith of all the people. The pastor's time and energy were multiplied many times over.

The genius of the Reformed tradition has been its refusal to become focused on the person of the pastor. The wise pastor will realize that it is good stewardship to develop the natural talents of the members, many of whom may know more about prayer than the pastor. These people can help to provide spiritual guidance to people who might never turn to the pastor. They often have a wisdom and discerning spirit that seem to come almost by instinct. Their own spiritual depth and innate understanding of the human spirit combine to make them "naturals." Martin Luther King, Jr., told a story about such a sensitive guide, who came up to him on a particularly trying day when he was drained of energy and called to him:

> I immediately went to her and hugged her affectionately. "Something is wrong with you," she said. "You didn't talk strong tonight." Seeking further to disguise my fears, I retorted, "Oh no, Mother Pollard, nothing is wrong. I am feeling as fine as ever." But her insight was discerning. "Now you can't fool me," she said. "I knows something is wrong. Is it that we ain't doing things to please you? Or is it that the white folks is bothering you?" Before I could respond, she looked directly into my eyes and said, "I don told you we is with you all the way." Then her face became radiant and she said in words of quiet certainty, "But even if we ain't with you, God's gonna take care of you." As she spoke these consoling words, everything in me quivered and quickened with the pulsing tremor of raw energy.[31]

This kind of direct, almost confrontational, spiritual counsel is probably best done by one's peers, by those who have nothing to gain or lose from being honest. The one quality that each of us needs in a relationship is that of utter honesty. We need to have people who can tell us the hard truth about ourselves, people we trust enough to be able to hear that truth even when it hurts.

The role of the elder or deacon in Reformed churches is

particularly suited for the kind of sponsorship of which Howard Thurman wrote, in which more mature Christians provide guidance for newer Christians and take some responsibility for their growth in grace. All too often, by neglecting this potential strength, we have turned people loose to fail without anyone to help them.

The services of the elders can multiply those of the pastor. Until the twentieth century, each elder had responsibility to examine communicants privately before each Communion service and to intervene so as to bring about reconciliation between neighbors found to be at odds with each other. Elders are vested with the authority of the congregation that has elected them. They can be chosen so that they possess the skills to be trusted counselors in times of personal need. They can also offer a guiding influence on a regular basis for a part of the congregation on a much more personal basis than the pastor, who is responsible for the whole congregation.

Group Guidance

Reformed Protestants developed another form of spiritual direction, the group. It could be either a small, covenant group or the whole congregation. Public sharing of spiritual experiences was a deep-seated part of the Puritan life. These groups were often the only way women could exercise leadership and discover mutual support. Cotton Mather paid high tribute to such a group: "I visited a society of devout Women, who were keeping this, as a day of private and solemn thanksgiving unto God. I prayed with them; and I preached to them, on 1 Sam. 2. 1. It may be, I am the only man in the World, that has preach'd unto such an auditory!"[32]

People were also encouraged to share their own religious experiences with the whole congregation. The importance of this sharing was that it knit the members together, assisting those who were going through trial or darkness of soul by exposing them to the light of the experiences of others. An excellent example of such a shared experience is that of Mary Barker, which was given before the Dublin congregation of John Rogers:

> I have great experiences of God, though at present I am not able to expresse them. I have been much afflicted for many years together in my relations, which for my sins have been taken from me; but the Lord who hath laid his hand heavy upon me, hath made me very sensible of my sins, and I have long lain under the burden of them; but the evidence of my pardon is, that the Lord hath removed the burden, and brought in the room his grace, and given me a heart to him-ward, and I have received much benefit by preaching, and praying, and reading in private and public, and by the preaching of Mr. Rogers I have received infinite good, and found great comforts by his showing how we might know Christ is in us of a truth; and by prayer which the Lord brought me earnestly into; the Lord made those means so useful to me, that I am much satisfied in the love of God to me, in Christ in me, who is all in all, and I do rest alone on Jesus Christ, for pardon and salvation by his blood.[33]

This testimony shows the women were encouraged to speak in public meeting among Puritans. It also shows the origin of the testimonial, which was later very widely developed among American Protestants and is still practiced in some conservative groups. Mutual strengthening and support from such a practice was a way by which the whole congregation assumed a role in the life of each member, while each member was responsible for a ministry to the whole.

Protestants have continued to use the guidance of small groups to supplement the one-to-one method. It is far less clerical and enables people to exercise their mutual ministry. This method was especially popular with continental pietists, who developed the art of group direction in their study-prayer groups, or conventicles. These frequently met on Sunday afternoons, in an effort to provide more spiritual nurture than could be found in the church service, which was geared to the needs of the masses and therefore to the religiously content. In these meetings, the sermon of the morning was discussed, people gave testimonies as to their own personal experiences of God's grace, and the implications of faith for daily life were mutually examined. There was shared prayer and exhortation of one another. Group guidance is a means of providing for the needs of many persons without draining the energy of a few.

In a variety of forms, Reformed Protestants have been given guidance for living their lives. They have used letters, personal sharing with friends, visitation by elders and pastors, pastoral counseling, and group direction. Some of these methods have been more important than others in particular periods of history, but all have played a role. Each has great potential today for helping people deal with the struggle to renew faith.

Reformed Qualities in Guidance

Whether the spiritual guide be a pastor, elder, another church member, or a group, there are some distinctively Reformed qualities to the relationship.

1. Reformed spiritual guidance is modest in its claims and very conscious of all human limitations. The sense of sin, so deeply a part of Reformed piety, frees the guide from the temptation to assume a role that is above the other person. As we grow in self-understanding, we recognize a shared sense of our frail and broken common humanity.

In any effort to provide guidance for another, the guide always stands alongside the other person. The guide must always be aware of weaknesses and woundedness in his or her self. Humility and the common sense of human sin lead to compassion and a refusal to look down on another person.

With humility we recognize our limits and know that we must entrust the real work of healing and spiritual growth to be done by God. Every guide must let go of a predetermined agenda for the other person. We do not often know what is best for that person, and we need to be very careful about trying to remake anyone according to our own expectations. As we return to consider our own failings, we should be able to reject the temptation to impose ourselves and our desires on the other.

Humility is also very important to help us be able to accept the most unacceptable qualities in the other person. If we are trying to help someone and we cannot accept the person as she or he is in the present, we should probably decline to engage in any relationship of depth, or we may do much damage. Such acceptance does not mean that guidance should be without concrete assistance or specific directions to the other person. Reformed guidance has at times been quite directive, not hesitating to call the other person to new levels of obedience and faith or fearing to disagree with something that is said. Anyone called to be a spiritual guide will, however, always be a sinner along with the other person, refusing to play god even when that role is tempting. When people seek out a guide, they look for someone who has traveled the road or is in the process of traveling it with them, but they also seek someone whose pilgrimage may be a bit farther along than their own so that the other person will have some wisdom to share with them.

2. Reformed spiritual guidance is egalitarian in spirit. The term "spiritual direction" has been somewhat foreign to Reformed Protestants because it suggests an authoritarian style, and Protestants have wanted to insist that it is God's grace and not human action that is the primary factor in spiritual development. The role of the guide is like that of a midwife, who assists the other in the process of giving birth to that which is seeking expression in the other's life. The whole of the spiritual life is really that of giving birth to Christ in our lives. That birth assumes different forms in different people. The midwife does not force birth to occur, but stands by and gently assists in an appropriate way as needed.

Although Protestants have turned to their pastors most often, the role of lay guides has been more important than is usually recognized, and it holds great potential for the multiplication of the pastor's effectiveness. In every congregation there are people who are spiritually mature, many of whom also have an innate understanding of human nature. The pastor may be able to suggest to these people the possibility that they have a calling, then help them to prepare and enable them to be available to others. Such a process would be a way of reviving the Reformed emphasis on the responsibility of all members for one another. As with deacons also, the use of elders is particularly well suited to Reformed practice of spiritual guidance. The elders have the spiritual life of the people as their primary responsibility. Surely some of these elders are spiritually mature enough to serve as guides for others. They need only a sense of this calling and some preparation for the responsibility of providing guidance for others.

3. The third quality is expectancy. We only give ourselves to those situations and persons in which we have hope. No one is likely to expend much energy with a person deemed hopeless. It is pointless to work for healing if one has no expectation of growth. That is why the spiritual guide must be a person who trusts that God wills for growth in the other person and that the process of providing guidance is cooperation with God's will. It is absolutely essential that both parties in any guidance relationship trust in God's grace to assist the process and hope that, in God, the other person *will* grow.

The Reformed emphasis on God's providence is a source of hope when the situation may otherwise offer few clues to a solution. One of the most difficult aspects of spiritual guidance is the danger of expecting too much and being disappointed, or even giving up, when great changes do not happen. Ben Campbell Johnson, a contemporary leader and writer in the area of spirituality among American Presbyterians, advises that we must learn to appreciate the small advances we make, because we cannot always even recognize our own growth. "We must be faithful and count on God to bring about the changes God wills for us."[34]

That is why prayer is so important for any kind of spiritual guidance. It helps if we begin each session with a time of quiet prayer, followed by a spoken prayer in which we seek for God's grace in the session. During the session

itself, it will often be necessary to pause, remind ourselves
of why we are here, and pray together. This is to ensure that
we do not become caught up in details that distract from
the central purpose of the session.

4. Reformed guidance deals with the whole of life, and
issues such as sexuality, relationships with parents or
spouse and children, physical health, employment, and
even money may come up, and they are never "beneath"
the dignity of the dialogue. They are related to the larger
end of the relationship, which is the person's growth in
relationship to God. All else needs to be seen and dealt with
in that light. Although spiritual guidance is not the same as
pastoral counseling, reformed guidance will not be fearful
of the insights of modern psychology. It is no accident of
history that the pastoral counseling movement has been
peopled by great numbers of Reformed Christians. The
tradition has always affirmed the importance of science and
welcomed the discoveries that the sciences make as contributions to a fuller and more complete understanding of the
human situation.

All spiritual guides do not have to have thorough psychological training, but they should have two qualities: (1)
They should know their limits and when to refer the other
person to a skilled professional. Without this respect for
limits, guidance can become therapy, and damage can be
done by the refusal to let go and turn the situation over to
someone with more competence and training. (2) They
should know enough about human nature to be aware of
common tendencies to avoid difficult subjects, especially
those dealing with sexuality, and should be prepared to
press with questions when appropriate.

5. The fifth quality is persistence. It means "standing
with" or "staying with" the other person. Our natural
tendency is to become too eager to see results, and in our
eagerness we get in the way of God's Spirit. First we must
learn to hear what the other is saying, and this will be not
only in words. It means that we must learn to pay close
attention to nonverbal clues and signs.

Any form of spiritual guidance takes time. It is not for

those who are too busy or for those who expect results in ten or twenty sessions. Because letter-writing has played such an important role in Reformed spiritual guidance, it must not be overlooked as one way of staying in touch with the other person in a highly mobile society. It enables a persistence to the relationship when it might otherwise be broken by geographic separation.

Becoming a Spiritual Guide

Bonhoeffer insisted that spiritual care was a requirement of the office of pastor, and to some extent that is true. Pastors are expected to be able to offer assistance to people in times of spiritual need and ought to be ready for these times to occur. On the other hand, no pastor should be too eager to become a spiritual guide. It takes a great investment of time to do this for another person. No pastor can possibly be the spiritual guide for very many parishioners without discovering that there is little time left for other necessary pastoral duties. Not all are equally well equipped to be spiritual guides, and not everyone should try. The most important clue that one may be called by God to the role of spiritual guide is when another person asks us to take on this responsibility. Even then it is important to be very careful to consider the matter prayerfully before saying our usually dutiful yes. Spiritual guidance not only takes a great deal of time; it takes a particular spiritual gift. It demands that one care very much about the other person.

We can assist only a very small number of people in this journey, and we can, of course, assist no one beyond that place that we ourselves have gone. *No one should be a spiritual guide who is not under guidance.* This comes as close to a general rule as can be made. It is necessary for all those who would offer guidance in the wilderness of the Christian life to be in a relationship of accountability in which their own lives are being opened to another, their own burdens shared, their personal problems faced. This practice keeps a would-be guide from becoming too confident, from losing touch with limitations, and from forgetting to be dependent upon the One who is the real guide, the Spirit of God.

The following are qualities that I believe must be present if one is to be engaged in spiritual guidance:

1. A deep and personal experience of Christian faith
2. Regular participation in a congregation
3. A disciplined form of private prayer
4. Some understanding about human psychology (not necessarily formal study of the subject)
5. Awareness of one's limitations, and motivations that are being regularly examined in a relationship of spiritual guidance
6. Some knowledge of and appreciation of the tradition of spiritual guidance in the life of the Christian church
7. A calling from God confirmed by others who seek you out
8. The willingness and ability to be honest with another person, especially when such honesty is painful

Spiritual guidance is not the same as counseling, although there are similarities. Counseling usually aims to deal with a particular problem that is causing some pain or anxiety for the other person. The counseling relationship is set up to come to some resolution through talking out the problem, dealing with its roots in one's personal history, and perhaps even acting out one's feelings. Professor Roy Fairchild, now emeritus professor of San Francisco Theological Seminary, who was the first person to hold a chair in Christian spirituality in a Reformed theological seminary, makes the distinction between counseling or therapy on the one hand and spiritual guidance or direction on the other by pointing out three distinct differences: spiritual guidance is not problem-centered, the client is not seen as regularly, and both the guide and the one guided are more dependent on the Holy Spirit than on each other.[35]

Another way of making the distinction is to say that a person comes to spiritual guidance in order to grow spiritually, not primarily in order to become more successful in marriage or more effective in dealing with co-workers.

Guidance and counseling may go on at the same time and complement each other, but there needs to be a clear understanding that they are different. If not, the spiritual guidance process will be dominated by therapy issues.

Each session of guidance begins with a time of quieting or centering in which the two people place themselves before God. There should be some brief quiet time, a time of shared prayer. There may be a time of confession which deals with failures, sin, guilt, and anxiety, but this should certainly be followed by a time of proclamation of forgiveness, perhaps making the sign of the cross on the forehead of the other person. All these acts establish with clarity the fact that the session is different from any kind of counseling session. It also establishes the fact that this session is related completely to God, who is central to the entire process. Without awareness of God's presence, the guidance session becomes another form of counseling, with less expertise and perhaps more theological jargon.

The primary subject matter of the guidance session is the life of the one who has come for help, as that life is examined from the perspective of God's grace. Thus there are some natural questions that will arise in the sessions, such as the following:

1. What signs are there of grace operating?
2. What is going on in the person's prayer life? Are there blocks?
3. What are the person's dominant images of God, and are they appropriate?
4. What are the person's spiritual experiences and expectations?
5. What about the person's dreams?
6. What are the faith issues that seem most real?
7. How is the person living out commitments to others?

Each of these should be uncovered, examined, acknowledged, and then held before God. The guide may point out particular ways in which the person may face these questions in the future, if the guide feels the confidence of having any wisdom on the subject.

To aid the healing and growing process, the guide will make positive suggestions about various "spiritual disciplines," which are ways through which we seek to become more attentive to ourselves and to God, such as:

1. Prayer
2. Journal-keeping
3. Meditation upon scripture
4. Silence
5. Fasting
6. Sacrificial work for others
7. Taking risks in faith, especially regarding important social issues

The necessary ingredients in the relationship include:

1. Trust in God's guidance. The contract to engage in spiritual guidance involves the willingness to pray for the other person regularly, both in the sessions and beyond them. It is in this way that the guide is open to the leading of the Spirit in trying to discern where the Spirit is leading the person.

2. Honesty. If the guide is trusted enough to be able to say the hard truth and be heard without defensiveness, then the relationship is likely to be fruitful. Defensiveness is a sign that such trust is not present. Bonhoeffer insists that the pastor or guide must press issues. For example, when someone indicates "I can't" in response to a suggestion, he says, "I surmise that the 'I can't' means, at bottom, 'I won't.' "[36] The guide may need to point this fact out clearly and without apology.

3. Kindness. Because the guide has such potential for harming the other person, there must be great care taken not to abuse that power by causing undue pain. Some pain may be essential if the person is to be helped, but the guide must discern the degree to which it is helpful. There is need for a delicate balance between law and gospel or obedience and forgiveness. Forgiveness without obedience can lead to taking grace for granted or hiding from hard truth. On the other hand, too rigorous a demand for obedience without a proclamation of forgiveness would drive a person to perplexity.

4. Respect for uniqueness. The temptation to impose our own way on the other is very great and must be resisted. The other person is special before God and must be treated as such. The duty of the guide is to observe, care for, and encourage the Spirit of God to work in the other person, not to try to shape that person in any predetermined way. Quick solutions are a temptation in our desire to "fix" things.

5. Attentiveness. We need to pay close attention to the other person. If our mind wanders from what is being presented, we are not caring for the person. If we are bored by the material being presented, it is better to say so and either redirect the conversation or, if the boredom continues, to end the relationship. It is honest to admit that we are not all suited for spiritual-guidance relationships with each other.

In spite of the individualism that has come to characterize American Protestantism, people need help in living wisely and faithfully. The Reformed tradition contains helpful practices which, if revived today, could assist the church in its ministry of care for its members. People could benefit from guided reflection upon their own spiritual journeys, whether in small groups or with one other person —pastor, elder, or friend.

> If you had a friend with whom you might now and then spend a little time, in conferring together, in opening your hearts, and presenting your unutterable groanings before God, it would be of excellent use: Such an one would greatly strengthen, bestead, and further you in your way to Heaven. Spend now and then (as occasions will permit) an hour (or so) with such a friend more than ordinary (sometimes a piece of a day, sometimes a whole day of extraordinary fast, in striving and wrestling with God for everlasting mercy.) And

be much in quickening conference, giving and taking mutual encouragements and directions in the matters of Heaven! Oh! the life of God that falls into the hearts of the Godly, in and by gracious Heavenly conference. Be open-hearted to one another, and stand one for another against the Devil and all his Angels. Make it thus your business in these and such like ways, to provide for Eternity.[37]

NOTES

1. Presbyterian Church (U.S.A.) *The Book of Confessions* (New York and Atlanta: Office of the General Assembly, 1983), 5.095.

2. *The Book of Confessions,* 5.136.

3. John Calvin, *Commentary on a Harmony of the Synoptic Gospels,* Matt. 18:15, vol. 2, p. 352.

4. Calvin, *Institutes of the Christian Religion,* ed. John T. McNeill, trans. Ford Lewis Battles (Philadelphia: Westminster Press, 1960), IV, XII, 8, p. 1236.

5. Calvin, *Institutes,* III, IV, 17, p. 642.

6. Calvin, *Institutes,* III, IV, 18, p. 643.

7. Calvin, *Institutes,* III, IV, 18, pp, 644–45.

8. Calvin, *Institutes,* III, IV, 14, p. 638.

9. Calvin, *Institutes,* III, IV, 12, p. 636.

10. Calvin, *Institutes,* III, IV, 12, p. 637.

11. Calvin, *Institutes,* III, IV, 14, pp. 638–39.

12. T. H. L. Parker, *John Calvin: A Biography* (Philadelphia: Westminster Press, 1975), p. 68.

13. Frederick Buechner, *The Final Beast* (San Francisco: Harper & Row, 1982), p. 115.

14. Elizabeth White, *The Experiences of God's Gracious Dealing with Mrs. Elizabeth White* (Boston: S. Kneeland and T. Green, 1741), p. 3.

15. White, *God's Gracious Dealing,* p. 5.

16. White, *God's Gracious Dealing,* p. 5.

17. White, *God's Gracious Dealing,* p. 7.

18. White, *God's Gracious Dealing,* p. 7.

19. White, *God's Gracious Dealing,* p. 14.

20. Richard Baxter, *The Reformed Pastor* (New York: Robert Carter & Brothers, 1860), p. 346.

21. Cotton Mather, *Diary of Cotton Mather,* ed. Worthington

Chauncey Ford (New York: Frederick Ungar Publishing Co., 1957), vol. 1, p. 240.

22. Francis Rous, "The Mystical Marriage," in *Treatises and Meditations* (London: Robert White, 1657), p. 702.

23. John Calvin, *The Letters of John Calvin,* comp. Jules Bonnet, trans. David Constable (Philadelphia: Presbyterian Board of Publications, n.d.), Jan. 8, 1549, vol. 2, p. 202.

24. John Calvin, *Letters,* Oct. 24, 1538, vol. 1, pp. 99–100.

25. John Calvin, *Letters,* Apr. 7, 1549, vol. 2, p. 216.

26. Samuel Rutherford, *Religious Letters* (Edinburgh and London: Anderson & Ferrier, 1894), pp. 407–08.

27. Rutherford, *Letters,* p. 293.

28. Calvin, *Institutes,* III, IV, 6, p. 630.

29. Howard Thurman, *With Head and Heart: The Autobiography of Howard Thurman* (New York: Harcourt Brace Jovanovich, 1979), p. 19.

30. Thurman, *With Head and Heart,* p. 20.

31. Martin Luther King, Jr., *Strength to Love,* in *A Martin Luther King Treasury* (Yonkers, N.Y.: Educational Heritage, 1964), p. 237.

32. Mather, *Diary,* vol. 1, p. 579.

33. Reported from John Rogers in *Obel or Beth-shemish,* by Patricia Caldwell, in *The Puritan Conversion Narrative* (New York: Cambridge University Press, 1983), p. 139.

34. Ben Campbell Johnson, *To Pray God's Will: Continuing the Journey* (Philadelphia: Westminster Press, 1987), p. 91.

35. Roy Fairchild, "Spiritual Direction in Pastoral Care: Guaranteed Not to Shrink," *Pacific Theological Review* 16 (Fall 1982): 3.

36. Dietrich Bonhoeffer, *Spiritual Care,* trans. Jay C. Rochelle (Philadelphia: Fortress Press, 1985), p. 41.

37. Jonathan Mitchel, "A Letter to His Friend," appended to *Discourse of the Glory,* 2nd ed. (London: J. Collins, 1677), pp. 15–16.

6

Practice:
Spirituality and Discipleship
in the World

Q. What does God forbid in the eighth commandment?
A. [God] forbids not only the theft and robbery which civil authorities punish, but God also labels as theft all wicked tricks and schemes by which we seek to get for ourselves our neighbor's goods, whether by force or under the pretext of right, such as false weights and measures, deceptive advertising or merchandising, counterfeit money, exorbitant interest, or any other means forbidden by God. He also forbids all greed and misuse and waste of his gifts.

The Heidelberg Catechism[1]

The Reformed tradition has produced people who are deeply concerned with matters of the interior life of the individual and, at the same time, with involvement in the affairs of the world. It has become a mark of the people called "Reformed" that they are active in the life of society, often making an impact far beyond their numbers. Involvement in local school boards, programs of social welfare, projects for better housing, or meeting the needs of senior citizens very often involve Reformed Christians in any community. Often they are the founders of the programs, and frequently they occupy significant positions of leadership.

This concern for the wider world is one that has also led

Reformed Christians to become involved in politics. Piety and politics are not always thought to go together. Many people see them as so incompatible that the truly spiritual people have nothing to do with the compromises and ambiguities that accompany any involvement in the political process. They are willing to leave politics to scoundrels. Reformed Christians, with important exceptions, have sought to put together their personal spiritual practices with their concern for the political order.

Calvin set the tone for a spirituality that was deeply concerned with affairs of state and nation. He began his *Institutes of the Christian Religion* with a preface to Francis I of France, in which he gave advice about the role of the Christian ruler and warned him of the dangers of misrule: "That king who in ruling over his realm does not serve God's glory exercises not kingly rule but brigandage."[2] He concluded the work with a chapter on "Civil Government," which he defends as the protector of order and thus a necessity for Christian faith and life. The civil government is appointed by God to provide us with essential "helps" during our earthly pilgrimage.[3] He believed that regular government and the ordering of society were so vital that when they are taken away, human life "differs little from the sustenance of cattle and of beasts of prey."[4]

At times, Calvin can appear extremely conservative in his attitude toward society, declaring, "With hearts inclined to reverence their rulers, the subjects should prove their obedience toward them, whether by obeying their proclamations, or by paying taxes, or by undertaking public offices and burdens which pertain to the common defense, or by executing any other commands of theirs."[5] He attacked the Anabaptists as revolutionaries and accused them of seeking to overturn God's established order. His belief in the necessity for order led him to go so far as to say that "the magistrate cannot be resisted without God being resisted at the same time."[6]

Yet Calvin also attacked with equal vigor those princes or rulers who he claimed "grow extravagantly insolent, indulge in luxury, swell with pride, and are intoxicated with the sweets of prosperity," and says that "if the Lord cannot tolerate such ingratitude, we need not be surprised. . . . The usual consequence is, that those whom God has raised to a high estate do not occupy it long."[7] He even attacked the people of Israel for putting up with the oppression of Roman rule. "The whole nation, I have lately showed, was so degenerate, that they chose rather to be oppressed with the yoke of tyranny, than to submit to any inconvenience arising from a change."[8]

Later Calvinists tended to follow Calvin in their suspicion of monarchs. The radical side of Calvin emerged in his commentary on the book of Daniel. He prepared the way for much later social upheaval: "For earthly princes lay aside all their power when they rise up against God, and are unworthy of being reckoned in the number of mankind. We ought rather utterly to defy than to obey them."[9]

One of the temptations of all monarchs, which Calvin finds most reprehensible, is that they "fabricate deities"[10] for the purpose of manipulating the faith of the people in these gods as a way of supporting their tyrannical rule. "They arm themselves with religion to strengthen their power, and pretend to encourage the worship of God for the single purpose of retaining the people in obedience."[11] Their use of religion as a prop to sustain their power is one that must be unmasked in order for the people to see that God cannot be so used. The loyalty of the people must be to God alone, and when monarchs abuse their power for self-seeking purposes the people need to be reminded that uncritical obedience to monarchs is a form of idolatry.

Calvin believed that the best form of government was a "system compounded of aristocracy and democracy," because it "is very rare for kings so to control themselves that their will never disagrees with what is just and right."[12] He believed that it was safer to have a number of people involved in government so as to balance out the self-interest of one another. No single individual should be trusted with too much power without other persons present who could challenge and check that claim to power. In this way, it was possible for a just society to be established.

Such a form of government required the services of many people who would be willing to involve themselves in the day-to-day operations of government. Calvin developed the idea of public service as a noble calling from God and "also the most sacred and by far the most honorable of all callings."[13] Those who have power and influence were urged by him to fulfill their duty to their fellow citizens as a duty toward God. The form of government that Calvin recommended required the talents and time of many people who were able to see their civic duty as an expression of their faith.

Calvin sought a middle ground between anarchy, which he understood as the result of making change in society too quickly, and tyranny, which came about through fear of challenging the power of the monarch. Calvin's carefully balanced tension between the extremes of rebellion and submission was difficult to maintain. He, himself, could go from one extreme to another. The Reformed confessions have tended to emphasize the duty to obey as primary. The Scots Confession says, "Therefore we confess and avow that those who resist the supreme powers, so long as they are acting in their own spheres, are resisting God's ordinance and cannot be held guiltless."[14] Yet even this contains a kind of permission to rebel because it ascribes limitations to the sphere of government. When the monarch oversteps these limits, then the Scots Confession may be read as permitting rebellion.

The Second Helvetic Confession expresses something of the same emphasis by saying first, "The Magistracy is from God. Magistracy of every kind is instituted by God himself for the peace and tranquillity of the human race, and thus it should have the chief place in the world."[15] But it goes on to describe the duties of the just magistrate, who must hold the Word of God and prevent anything contrary from being taught. Furthermore the monarch has the clear duties to "protect widows, orphans and the afflicted" and to avoid accepting bribes.[16] Those monarchs who neglect their duty have, it may be construed, surrendered their right to rule. The people may rebel against rulers who do not accept their responsibility to rule with justice. This implied permission to rebel against tyrants has inspired Calvinists throughout history. The writers of the Scots Confession were, themselves, engaged in a rebellion against the English, which would continue for a century until they won their independence in religion and their right to participate in their own government. Calvinism has always lived in tension with monarchy in any form. The Reformed tradition has been frequently critical of monarchs and ready to overthrow them. It has thus involved people in political action as part of their religious duty.

Such political activism by people from the Reformed tradition has been common throughout history. The Dutch used their spiritual resources to throw off the Spanish conquerors; the Puritans prayed and fought against the monarch in England; the Scots found courage in their faith to resist the power of the English monarchy; and the American Revolution was itself dubbed the "Presbyterian rebellion" by King George III.

In the period of Nazi rule in twentieth-century Germany, leaders of the "Confessing Church" gathered to declare their faith over against the official German Evangelical Church. They rejected the ways in which the state church had compromised its life and message to accommodate itself to Nazi restrictions. The Theological Declaration of Barmen stated the Reformed principle of denial of ultimate authority to the civil government in several clear statements. Among them is the following: "We reject the false doctrine, as though there were areas of our life in which we would not belong to Jesus Christ, but to other lords—areas in which we would not need justification and sanctification through him."[17]

In spite of this long tradition of suspicion of state power and encouragement for Christians to take responsibility for keeping state power limited and just, the Reformed tradition has not lived comfortably with its heritage. Within the last hundred years, American Protestantism has been deeply divided between those who have emphasized the Christian life as primarily a private inner journey of personal morality, prayer, devotional experiences, and a sense of closeness to God and those who have felt called to take up the outer journey of discipleship by seeking to change society, writing letters to governmental officials, and trying to get unjust laws changed by protest or civil disobedience.

The division between these two groups is relatively new for Presbyterians. In the eighteenth century, the major conflicts were between those who accepted the Great Awakening, with its emphasis on the experience of God, on the one hand and those who insisted on rigid doctrinal orthodoxy on the other. Both sides were concerned with the works of justice and understood the spiritual life to include doing as well as being. Until the period immediately preceding the Civil War, there was a fairly consistent relationship between personal piety and actions that sought to bring about justice.

The struggles of the church to come to terms with the issue of slavery brought about a different alignment, which has produced a great deal of suspicion and anger on the part of people on both sides of the gulf. The abolition movement made a clear connection between conversion and embracing the cause of freeing the slaves. The reaction to this connection was expressed as the attempt to privatize the experience of God so that it could be maintained with no relationship to the issues of the world, especially the issue of slavery. This division led to the impoverishment of the witness of the church, as people chose sides and saw the choice as an either/or. Both the inner and outer paths have at times become fragmented and distorted. It should be added that because the issue of race was the central issue in bringing American Protestantism to this division, the black church is a continuing witness to the white church that spirituality must include discipleship in the world and must not be limited to the personal and private side of life.

The conflict over slavery brought about the articulation of the doctrine of the "spirituality of the church." This argument for support of the status quo was originally a defense against dealing with the explosive and potentially divisive issue of abolition. Especially for southern Presbyterians, but with a pervasive power that still affects us all, this idea meant that the church should leave alone any involvement in the issues of society, with the possible exception of those relating to personal morality such as temperance, gambling, and marital fidelity.

This attitude produced a privatistic pietism which limited itself to a personal world of spiritual matters and, in its extreme, rejected contamination with the sinful world and all its problems. The evil "secular" world was to be avoided, and was certainly not a primary arena for faith. Christians could concentrate on their own inner journey with Christ as a means of escape from involvement with the sordid and fallen world. People could seek peace with God in prayer, and this way of life could be a way of being alone with the Lord, nurturing the soul, deepening faith, and sensing the strength of that relationship as something joyous and powerful. The primary task of the church was that of bringing others to a saving faith and of strengthening the faith of those already in the membership. It was a task of rescuing people from the fallen world.

This "spiritual" form of Christianity has often meant a rejection of certain kinds of sin, usually the blatant kinds of personal wrongdoing that are connected with people other than ourselves. The sins that cause the greatest consternation are matters of private morality such as those that pertain to the use or abuse of one's sexuality. Thus, the scriptures may be read quite selectively so as to pronounce God's judgment on fornication, adultery, and homosexuality but be played down or ignored when they denounce lending money for interest, greed, gluttony, national pride, or war. Sins that have great impact on other people are of far less concern than sins committed in private. Such an attitude is personified by those who denounce abortion as "anti-life" but oppose gun control, sex education, or publicly funded prenatal clinics and demand the reintroduction of the death penalty as the Lord's vengeance upon the wicked.

In reaction to the narrow and insular pharisaical piety of much of conservative Protestantism, the "liberal" wing of the church chose to live out faith in deeds instead of words, in action instead of prayer. The activists turned away from what they perceived to be an antihuman, antiphysical, antipolitical perversion of the gospel, which turns its back on the needs of the world in order to pluck souls from contamination by the evil world. The prophetic form of witnessing to our faith in the world demands that we deal with economic systems, racism and sexism, the exploitation of the poor, the oppression of unjust governments, and the threat of nuclear war. Unfortunately the activists have also rejected much of the power of the nurturing tradition in the process. In the name of the affirmation of life, they have seen prayer as otherworldly and all traditional forms of piety as escape from the world in which Christ calls us to live and act.

The activists have generally seen the pietists as petty, narrow, and legalistic, and the pietists have seen the activists as strident, unconcerned about the saving power of Christ, and more interested in secular politics than in salvation. Both sides have made exaggerations of each other's positions so that they could dismiss any possible need to take each other seriously.

The trap for the activists has been that of an almost paranoid fear of religious experience, and sometimes even avoidance of religious language. This has led to losing touch with the source of strength and motivation for their action in the world. A faith without the sustaining power of prayer and a sense of God's presence can become weary and discouraged. It can be turned from idealism into bitterness and despair.

Our nation has many burned-out activists who no longer function as prophets, often having adjusted to the world. Some, in cynical fashion, become quite successful in the very activities they once attacked, becoming stockbrokers

or investment bankers, for example. Frequently they have
abandoned the church entirely in order to function in a
purely secular world. There is good reason to suspect that
the membership losses of mainstream Protestant churches
actually represent considerably larger numbers of these
former activists than of angry conservatives. They have left,
not in strident protest and taking large pledges with them;
they have simply become bored and tired and quit. The
Presbyterian Church Membership Survey of several years
ago pointed out that most former church members do not
now attend any church. They have left church membership
and activity. Having been worn out or simply discouraged
and bored, they have given up the struggle.

Our debt to the activists is real. Without them and their
persistence, there is great likelihood that the church would
be little more than a haven for those who want nothing to
do with the world. There is a natural tendency for the
church to draw in upon itself, seeing itself as over against
the world and concentrating on good feelings at the expense
of doing anything that might call into question values that
make us comfortable. The activists have been God's gift to
save the church from withdrawal by insisting that "faith
without works is dead."

Yet activism without roots in personal piety can easily
degenerate into a self-righteous pride in good works, filled
with anger at those who cannot or will not agree. It is eager
to pass judgment, but is almost totally unable to speak
comfort to wounded people. Calvin, in his commentary on
the book of Daniel, says that the works of righteousness
often are not successful because well-meaning people become too self-confident. "Hence it is not surprising if those
who undertake good causes often fail of success, as we often
see among the profane. . . . As ambition seized them, they
became pleased with their own plans."[18] This has been the
problem of activism without a deep personal faith to
undergird its projects. Grand plans and glorious ideals
become the source of terrible disillusionment when things
do not turn out as expected. Without a vision and source of
sustenance beyond immediate goals, there is no ground for

staying with a cause when it is no longer popular or satisfying.

Prayer and politics are inseparable if either is to have real integrity. Jonathan Edwards saw in his own day the danger of the split between personal piety and the works of justice that we experience today in modern Protestantism:

> Some men shew a love to others as to their outward man, they are liberal of their worldly substance, and often give to the poor; but have no love to, or concern for the souls of men. Others pretend a great love to men's souls, that are not compassionate and charitable towards their bodies. The making a great shew of love, pity, and distress for souls, costs 'em nothing; but in order to shew mercy to men's bodies, they must part with money out of their pockets. But a true Christian love to our brethren, extends both to their souls and bodies.[19]

There are signs of healing today in American Protestantism. The so-called "evangelical" sector is in the process of revolution from within. The Declaration of Social Concern signed in Chicago in 1971 contained a ringing call to evangelicals to attack American materialism and the unfair distribution of the world's wealth. The Sojourners' Community has become an important voice for this new awakening within evangelical Protestantism, and names such as Ronald Sider, John Howard Yoder, and Jim Wallis are significant.

Protestant liberals have also moved toward a recovery of wholeness and a search for renewal of the spirit. Discouragement with the failure of many of their idealistic programs to become realized has been an important motivation for a new openness to the inward journey of prayer. Oppressive structures have been remarkably resistant to the denunciations and energies of modern prophets. It is very difficult to see progress in the struggle for equality and justice. Racism continues to rear its ugly head just when we had thought it dead. The poor become poorer and the rich become richer in spite of laws meant to distribute wealth more equitably. In order for liberals to continue to struggle to right the wrongs of our world, they must have motivation beyond the results they can actually see. It might be a cause for celebration if great numbers of people in our churches today were really serious about their personal piety or about their witness to justice. The reality is that, more often, the great majority are neither very fervent about prayer nor very courageous about bearing witness in the public arena. Discomfort and fear of both activities produce a kind of dead goodness, which is dutiful in the avoidance of flagrant personal immorality. It strives for decency but has no passion, no sense of being grasped by the living Christ, and no sense of complicity in the evil of the world. Such people may be kind, comfortable, and successful, but they are almost completely without awareness of the need for mystery in their lives. Edwards envisioned the power of a total commitment to the gospel, which requires a proper balance of the external duties of devotion and the moral duties in society. He proclaimed the possibility of a true wholeness of Christian witness with this declaration:

> If God's people in this land, were once brought to abound in such deeds of love, as much as in praying, hearing, singing, and religious meetings and conference, it would be a most blessed omen: there is nothing would have a greater tendency to bring the God of love down from heaven to the earth: so amiable would be the sight, in the eyes of our loving and exalted Redeemer, that it would soon as it were fetch him down from his throne in heaven, to set up his tabernacle with men on the earth, and dwell with them.[20]

The need of the church today is for a spirituality that combines a deep and renewed personal piety with a passionate concern for the world. Piety without world concern gets reduced to sentimentalism and the pursuit of experiences aimed at making the individual feel happier or more adjusted, more content, and at peace within. Such religion becomes truly the opiate of the people; it numbs them to the heartbreak of much of the world. Words and deeds must go together. Words take on credibility when they are accompanied by actions that are congruous with them. Our deeds help us to interpret our own vocabulary. As we act in the world, words like salvation, forgiveness, grace, and compassion are enfleshed by our experience with other people. Yet matching words with deeds is not easy. It requires a great deal of sacrifice, and most of us would rather avoid such a demand.

At the center of our difficulty is discomfort with the material world and the separation of the material from the spiritual. It is a constant temptation for Christians to reject the world that God has created as somehow inferior to a spiritual world of their own creation. A faith that holds the incarnation to be central ought to be protected from such a separation. The incarnation is the basis both for true Christian piety and for passionate concern for justice in the world of the flesh. It enables us to see God's love for us in the most personal way, and it forces us to take with the utmost seriousness every other human being.

Because of Jesus Christ, humanity is inseparably linked with God. He is the bridge across the chasm that otherwise divides one from the other. To the extent that we participate in the living Christ who dwells in the believer's heart and soul, we are made to participate in the reality of the divine nature. Calvin put it this way:

> For we await salvation from him not because he appears to us afar off, but because he makes us, ingrafted into his body, participants not only in all his benefits but also in himself. . . . Not only does he cleave to us by an indivisible bond of fellowship, but with a wonderful communion, day by day, he grows more and more into one body with us, until he becomes completely one with us.[21]

Our participation in the living Christ means that all human life takes on a sacred quality. The unity of flesh and spirit in Christ is the basis for taking all that is human with utmost reverence. To believe in the incarnation is to accept every human being as an image, however marred and distorted, of Christ. No one can be treated with contempt;

no person can be ignored; no human situation is beneath Christian concern. The way we treat other people frequently says more about what we believe than our words.

The world around us is completely changed by the incarnation, and we are enabled to see everything in a new way when we view it as those who believe that God saw fit to live here in the person of Jesus. He enhances all life because he was born of a woman, slept, ate, felt pain and sorrow, and was touched by and loved other human beings. He wept at the grave of Lazarus and enjoyed the companionship of others in festivity. Nothing human is alien to the God who was in Christ. Everything human has the possibility of revealing the divine.

This is the way we are to behold other people. Calvin recognized that the command to love was universal in its scope, which goes far beyond those we know and see with our own eyes.

> We cannot but behold, as in a mirror, our own face in those who are poor and despised, who have come to an end of their own power to help themselves, and who groan under their burden, even though they are utter strangers to us. Even in dealing with a Moor or a Barbarian, from the very fact of his being a man, he carries about with him a looking-glass in which we can see that he is our brother and our neighbour.[22]

In spite of the limitation of gender in these words, the clear implication is that we are to treat all other people, familiar or not, as neighbors; we are to see in them the face of the Christ.

To be human is to share in the nature of the God who was in Christ. Much that passes for Christian piety is a distortion because it demeans the physical world and rejects the gift that God gives. It acts as if the incarnation never took place. It is possible to have spiritual experiences that are not authentic. A warm heart is no evidence that we have encountered God. We can be deceived by our own deep-seated needs so that we are incapable of discerning what is going on. Our personal experience of new life in Christ must produce results in practice. When we have met the living Christ we are more loving, more accepting, more forgiving, and more willing to involve ourselves in concern for others. If encounters with God lead a person away from other people, then it is necessary to ask if that person has really encountered Christ. Edwards puts it bluntly:

> Passing affections easily produce words; and words are cheap; and godliness is more easily feigned in words than in actions. Christian practice is a costly laborious thing. The self-denial that is required of Christians, and the narrowness of the way that leads to life, don't consist in words, but in practice. . . . Thus it is plain that Christian practice is the best sign or manifestation of the true godliness of a professing Christian.[23]

Christ is always the One for others. His whole life was spent in service to the least desirable, the least acceptable or reputable. He sought out the poor and needy as those to whom he had been sent. The biblical record makes clear that God loves the poor with a special passion. The poor are not more moral or more deserving, but they need God's love most. What has been called "God's preferential option for the poor" among twentieth-century liberation theologians was prefigured when Calvin wrote, "In short, though God pours forth his grace on the rich in common with the poor, yet his will is to prefer these to those, that the mighty might learn not to flatter themselves, and that the ignoble and the obscure might ascribe all that they are to the mercy of God, and that both might be trained up to meekness and humility."[24]

Any experience of Christ that does not lead us to share his passionate concern for others is misunderstood or simply imagined no matter how powerful or life-changing it may be. If, on the other hand, our experience of Christ leads us to a regard for others and a willingness to risk time and energy in the service of human need, then that experience has met the primary test of authenticity. Spiritual experience is the liberation of the self from preoccupation with itself. It is the beginning of freedom to care about others with abandon. It is, after all, self-preoccupation that keeps us from noticing the pain of the other.

God is love, and the experience of God's love is one that meets our basic need for love so that we can be free to love others. Without receiving love, we cannot love others, no matter how hard we try. That is why spiritual experience is so linked with self-giving love for others. The heart of the experience of God is an inner knowing that "I am loved, loved beyond comprehension, beyond my earning or deserving." This deep knowing of the soul is the shattering of the otherwise inexhaustible need for love, which drives us to keep ourselves in the very center of the universe and to evaluate everything on the basis of how much it meets our needs. The person who knows love is able to love; the person who has been in the presence of the Divine Lover is filled to the brim with a sense of satisfaction of that need and can let go and share love. That is why truly great mystics are always such powerful figures and are often revolutionary. They have a vision of how things might be that is not blurred by fear of what might happen to them. They are powerful because their vision has broken down their need for being loved. They have been liberated from their own inner needs, and they are empowered to go out and challenge the powers of evil in the world. They know, from their own experience, that the power of evil within them has been broken by the power of God's love.

Christian love operates in two different ways: The first is the face-to-face way, which is most clearly acted out in the parable of the good Samaritan. It is an attitude toward the neighbor in our presence who is in need. It is the willingness to act in regard for that neighbor. This personal, one-to-one way of love seeks to be kind, forgiving, helping, caring, and healing in all our relationships. It is an essential mark of the Christian life. No one can claim to be an obedient disciple of Christ whose personal relationships are without any evidence of kindness or concern for the well-being of others. The prophet who denounces evil everywhere but is a beast to spouse and children at home, is a phony. The one who cares about South Africa with great vigor but who treats fellow workers like trash is without the central mark of the Christian life. Love for humanity in general without caring for the particular people who are within arm's reach is not real love.

The second way of love is more long-range. It does not lead immediately and directly to personal encounter with other people, and does not satisfy our need for affirmation that we are, in fact, engaged in being loving. Long-range love is acted out in the way we deal with the structures of society and exercise our love to transform those structures. This second path leads to the arena of politics, because only in this way can people who are hungry get fed and people who are homeless find shelter. This form of love is as inescapable as the first. We cannot love people as Christ loved them and ignore those needs which cannot be addressed by our own private compassion for those we happen to meet.

Calvin addressed the significance of long-range love when he wrote about the meaning of the neighbor:

> Since Christ has shown in the parable of the Samaritan that the term "neighbor" includes even the most remote person, we are not expected to limit the precept of love to those in close relationships. . . . We ought to embrace the whole human race without exception in a single feeling of love; here there is no distinction between barbarian and Greek, worthy and unworthy, friend and enemy, since all should be contemplated in God, not in themselves.[25]

Short-range love is not enough. It leaves untouched the urgent need of most of the people of the world who suffer want, are deprived of dignity, are without meaningful employment, who go to bed hungry, spend their lives in refugee or detention centers, or are locked in prisons or simply left by themselves without human touch. Long-range love requires that we move beyond immediate concerns in order to care about those whose lives are destroyed by public or national policies. The need for more than short-range love can be made most clear by reflecting that if the good Samaritan frequented the road to Jericho and if he found himself confronted again and again by people who had been beaten and robbed along that road and did nothing more than offer personal aid and comfort to the victims, he would be naive, to say the least. He must begin to make some connection between the frequency of beatings and robberies along that road and the lack of proper police protection, as well as the high unemployment or poverty in the area which drives people to criminal acts. Christ calls us to love beyond our immediate touch.

Most Christians agree that prayer and deeds of compassion and mercy belong together as two parts of the Christian life. We may disagree about the weight to be given each in the balance of faithfulness. But the real question is, how do our inner life of prayer and our outer life of concern for others come together? How does this happen in concrete situations? How do we balance these two parts of our lives? Of course, there will be different paths for each person, but there are some common patterns.

1. We can be energized and motivated by our personal experience of God, so that we have both the vision and the strength to go out and engage in acts of risk-taking on behalf of others. Our own experience becomes the source for our motivation for involvement with others. Our freedom from self-centeredness is freedom to care more fully for them. As we are met by God's love, we are compelled to share that love by our actions. Thus our prayer becomes the force that empowers us to engage the world. We move back and forth between being renewed in silence and quiet by ourselves, reading the Bible and praying, and then carrying that new energy out into the world with vigor. This back-and-forth pattern is a central way in which the spiritual experience of the individual is related to the activity of the disciple. The movement back and forth may be daily or weekly, or it may follow some other pattern. Some people are so heavily involved with the world that they find it necessary to take a day a month for personal retreat.

Dr. Martin Luther King, Jr., wrote a graphic description of this need for strength to deal with the struggles of his active witness:

> It seemed that all of my fears had come down on me at once. I had reached the saturation point. . . . In this state of exhaustion, when my courage had almost gone, I determined to take my problem to God. My head in my hands, I bowed over the kitchen table and prayed aloud. . . . At that moment I experienced the presence of the Divine as I had never before experienced him. . . . Almost at once my fears began to pass from me. My uncertainty disappeared. I was ready to face anything. The outer situation remained the same, but God had given me an inner calm.[26]

Because Dr. King was so deeply involved in the civil rights movement and because so much of his energy was needed to provide the critical leadership that the movement required, he was in constant danger of running dry, of becoming bitter, or of surrendering to despair. He needed prayer to keep going. To the extent that the rest of us are committed to any cause that demands great amounts of our energy, we share his need for regular times of renewal to keep going.

Yet neither the times of quiet nor the times of activity should be seen exclusively in relation to their opposites. Each has its own integrity, and each is a form of spirituality. Each also has its function to provide wholeness and balance. Robert McAfee Brown warns that "what happens in the experience of 'withdrawal' *can* have meaning in and of itself. That is to say, it is not to be valued only in terms of its utility for a subsequently invigorated life."[27] Even though each activity has its own integrity and value, each activity will strengthen and enhance the other. The more vigorous and risky our action in the world, the more we will need quiet time. One reason that many people do not seem to require retreats is that they are living in a state of semiconsciousness; they are not giving of themselves to any cause with real enthusiasm.

2. A second form of connection between the inner and outer forms of our discipleship is the way our experience of

God alters our way of knowing and seeing. All of us are creatures of our culture. We are shaped by its values more than we know. We are captive to its peculiar way of seeing the world. The possibility open to us all is that we can become new creatures in Christ. As God unites us in mystical union to Jesus Christ, we are made able to pierce through the lies that otherwise hold us captive. We become, by God's grace, new creatures who are not bound by the limited vision of the world. We can comprehend the world with a fresh understanding and be open to new possibilities, where before we saw only limitations of what we thought natural.

As our vision is renewed and clarified, the will of God becomes clearer for us. In the same process in which the will of God is clarified, the evil of the world also becomes more clear. It is by stepping back from our frantic activity in the world that we can see the world with eyes that are not clouded by our own desires or fears.

Prayer creates distance from the world. We step away from our usual activities in order to gain new insight. We remove ourselves from the rush of activity so that our actions may be better channeled to be in accordance with God's direction. Dorothee Soelle describes our slavery to modern Western society as our inability to question its presuppositions about the centrality of production and distribution, and she declares that "to meditate means neither to produce nor to consume. Nor does it mean to make oneself fit for further production and consumption."[28] As our wills become conformed to the will of God, we discover the hypocrisy of the world, the ugliness of society, the betrayals of truth that are taken for granted. In short, to the extent that we allow prayer to become a two-way process, God will remove the blinders from our eyes and we will see differently. Such new vision will also lead us to act in the world as agents of God.

3. A third connection between prayer and action is that of discovering the presence of God in places we least expect. We may discover that our most significant moments of closeness with God occur, not in prayer or meditation when

we are by ourselves, but in the midst of ministry to others. We learn that we are not alone, no matter how far removed from the realm we call "sacred" we may be. Our action in the world is performed as those who work in the company of the Crucified One, who goes with us into life's darkest places. Those who seek after Christ will be met in the heart of darkness and suffering—in the midst of pain, and not in avoidance of it!

Those who would find Christ must deal with their own fear of pain. Once we have come to this awareness, we will be less afraid of being hurt. Fear of being alone and isolated, fear of being ridiculed, fear of pain—these can destroy any witness we make. They can make cowards of us all. Above all, it is the fear of death that holds us and restrains us from being our best selves. Calvin wrote of this difficulty "that many who boast themselves Christians are gripped by such a great fear of death, rather than a desire for it, that they tremble at the least mention of it, as of something utterly dire and disastrous. . . . No one has made progress in the school of Christ who does not joyfully await the day of death and final resurrection."[29] We meet the pain of others without being self-righteous or discouraged because we know that Love is stronger than evil. Death is swallowed up in victory, and life cannot be defeated by death's power.

4. To know the power of Christ is to recognize Christ in the hurts of others wherever they may be. After explaining how the women cared for Christ during his ministry, Edwards goes on to speak about our situation: "Though we cannot now be charitable in this way, to Christ in person, who, in his exalted state, is infinitely above the need of our charity; yet we may be charitable to Christ now, as well as they then; for though Christ is not here, yet he has left others in his room, to be his receivers; and they are the poor."[30]

As Christ suffers even now with the earth's victims, we are able to recognize him in them and to share in his suffering as, in some small measure, we share in their suffering. This is the meaning of taking up our own cross and following him. Calvin says that as we meet and deal with other people, we are not to think about whatever merit they may have in themselves: "Look upon the image of God" in them, "to which we owe all honor and love." Therefore, we have no reason to refuse to help anyone we meet who needs our aid. The fact that the other person does not deserve our aid is no excuse: "the image of God" is what recommends that person to us.[31] We can see the face of Christ in the face of a peasant in Central America, the nameless, faceless slum dweller in an American city, or in the Southeast Asian refugee.

As Christ touches all of life in the power of his life, we are caught up in his overarching love for everything and everyone. As we reach out to those who need our help, we may discover that our faith is strengthened as our sense of being in the presence of Christ is revived. We become more Christlike as we take up the cross of those around us and assist in the bearing of it.

Encounter with Christ is the basis for our own willingness to take every other human being seriously as sister or brother and so to work for their fullness of life. Deep spiritual experience is, therefore, frequently very disturbing, for it enhances our awareness of suffering in all creation. People who claim to have had an experience of Christ that made them feel just wonderful and full of goose bumps may well be imagining a Christ of their own making. One cannot be lifted up to the heights of God's love without becoming aware of the tragic condition of the world.

The experience of God in which we see ourselves honestly is the experience of knowing that we share much with all other people in the world. That sharing includes recognizing their emptiness and ugliness in ourselves. We are not above or beyond the very sins we most abhor in others. The first experiences of Christ's love may be glorious, but it goes on from there. It takes us deeper into ourselves and forces us to admit that all of what we find there is not pleasant. We are presented with challenges we would much rather avoid and demands that seem impossible. Yet genuine experience of God is of such a persuasive power that it draws us to say yes to that which we fear and shun. The gift of the presence of God is costly, and only as we dare to follow where we are led do we discover both the cost and the joy of the pilgrimage of faith.

5. The fifth connection between our inner and outer lives is in our ability to persist when the going gets rough. Despair and cynicism are particularly alluring temptations for us in our culture. We are accustomed to having things happen quickly, and when the social conditions against which we struggle do not appear to be changing and our efforts seem to be in vain, we can either become cynical, giving in to despair, or we can wear out, getting tired of a particular cause and going on to another cause more in vogue. The deeper our commitment, the more we may experience such disillusionment. To sustain commitment to a cause when we do not see the results is very difficult. Our convictions need to be upheld by an inner strength.

The Reformed emphasis on the providence of God has been an aid for those who are tempted to give up. Providence has been misunderstood as an objective reality apart from human experience. In actuality, providence is another way of speaking of grace. Calvin speaks about the importance of providence as a means of encouragement when we might give up. "Here is our only ground for firmness and confidence: in order to free us of all fear and render us victorious amid so many dangers, snares, and mortal struggles, [Christ] promises that whatever the Father has entrusted into his keeping will be safe."[32] Such a conviction is not a human possibility. It is a gift of God's grace.

Our present experiences of Christ's presence in our lives and the memory of those experiences in the past become the basis for our confidence in that loving presence in the moment of temptation and doubt. It enables us to sustain our commitments when otherwise we could not continue without being overwhelmed by a sense of defeat. The Westminster Shorter Catechism, answering the question, "What are the benefits which in this life do accompany or flow from justification, adoption, and sanctification?" responds, "The benefits which in this life do accompany or flow from justification, adoption, and sanctification are: assurance of God's love, peace of conscience, joy in the Holy Ghost, increase of grace, and perseverance therein to the end."[33]

When we pray, we put ourselves before God and we dare to allow God to renew us, reform us, and free us from our anxieties. We do not know ahead of time what God will do with us or how God will lead us or even where God will send us. Prayer is the radical act of trusting God without knowing how God will deal with us. That is why trust is of the essence in our relationship with God. This trust is the basis for all inner calm, and thus for our persistence in doing justice in the world. It enables us to endure disappointment without despair; it fortifies us for those times when there is little evidence that our best efforts are getting anywhere; it keeps us going when faith grows dim and the price of our obedience and faithfulness seems too high. Good intentions and resolutions are not good enough. Charles Hodge said that the holiness is not brought about "by the force of conscience, nor of moral motives, nor by acts of discipline, but by being united to Christ so as to become reconciled to God, and partakers of the Holy Ghost."[34]

A personal relationship with Jesus Christ is the basis for our ability to carry on. It is the inner persuasion that we can remain faithful in spite of risks, discouragements, lack of results, and opposition. Paul closes his great prison letter with a personal confession of how God has strengthened him: "For I have learned to be content with whatever I have. I know what it is to have little, and I know what it is to have plenty. In any and all circumstances I have learned the secret of being well-fed and of going hungry, of having plenty and of being in need" (Phil. 4:11–12). All of us may not have to face the same terrible hostility that Paul faced, but we can identify with him, for we too face hunger for results, want for evidence of success, and the abasement of having our friends call us naive or foolish. The promise of the Christian life is not that things will go well for us, but that in the midst of the darkness we will be able to endure.

Grant, Almighty God, that as thou hast adopted us for this end, that we may show brotherly kindness one toward another and labor for our mutual benefit,—O grant, that we may prove by the whole tenor of our life that we have not been called in vain by thee, but that we may live so in harmony with each other that integrity and innocence may prevail among us; and may we so strive to benefit one another, that thy name may be thus glorified by us, until having at length finished our course, we reach the goal which thou hast set before us, that having at last gone through all the evils of this life, we may come to that blessed rest which has been prepared for us in heaven by Christ our Lord. Amen.

John Calvin[35]

NOTES

1. Presbyterian Church (U.S.A.), *The Book of Confessions* (New York and Atlanta: Office of the General Assembly, 1983), 4.110.

2. Calvin, *Institutes of the Christian Religion,* ed. John T. McNeill, trans. Ford Lewis Battles (Philadelphia: Westminster Press, 1960), Preface, p. 12.

3. Calvin, *Institutes,* IV, XX, 2, p. 1487.

4. Calvin, *Commentary on the Book of the Prophet Isaiah,* trans. William Pringle (Grand Rapids: Baker Book House, 1984), 24:2, vol. 1, p. 167.

5. Calvin, *Institutes,* IV, XX, 23, p. 1510.

6. Calvin, *Institutes,* IV, XX, 23, p. 1511.

7. Calvin, *Commentary on a Harmony of the Evangelists,* trans. William Pringle (Grand Rapids: Wm. B. Eerdmans Publishing Co., 1949), Luke 1:52, vol. 1, pp. 59–60.

8. Calvin, *Harmony of Evangelists,* Matthew 2:9, vol. 1, p. 136.

9. Calvin, *Commentaries: The Book of Daniel,* trans. Thomas Myers (Grand Rapids: Baker Book House, 1984), 6:23, vol. 1, p. 382.

10. Calvin, *Daniel,* 3:3–7, vol. 1, p. 205.

11. Calvin, *Daniel,* 3:8–12, vol. 1, p. 214.

12. Calvin, *Institutes,* IV, XX, 8, p. 1493.

13. Calvin, *Institutes,* IV, XX, 4, p. 1490.

14. *Book of Confessions,* 3.24.

15. *Book of Confessions,* 5.252.

16. *Book of Confessions,* 5.254.

17. *Book of Confessions,* 8.15.

18. Calvin, *Daniel,* 6:23, vol. 1, p. 383.

19. Jonathan Edwards, *Religious Affections,* ed. John E. Smith (New Haven, Conn.: Yale University Press, 1959), p. 369.

20. Jonathan Edwards, "Thoughts on the Revival of Religion in New England," in *Edwards on Revivals* (New York: Dunning & Spaulding, 1832), p. 409.

21. Calvin, *Institutes,* III, II, 24, pp. 570–71.

22. Calvin, "Sermon on Galatians 6:9–11," in Ronald S. Wallace, *Calvin's Doctrine of the Christian Life* (Grand Rapids: Wm. B. Eerdmans Publishing Co., 1959), p. 150.

23. Edwards, *Religious Affections,* p. 411.

24. Calvin, *Commentaries on the Catholic Epistles,* trans. and ed. John Owen (Grand Rapids: Baker Book House, 1984), James 2:5, p. 303.

25. Calvin, *Institutes,* II, VIII, 55, pp. 418–19.

26. Martin Luther King, Jr., *Strength to Love,* in *A Martin Luther King Treasury* (Yonkers, N.Y.: Educational Heritage, 1964), p. 229.

27. Robert McAfee Brown, *Spirituality and Liberation* (Philadelphia: Westminster Press, 1988), p. 46.

28. Dorothee Soelle, *Death by Bread Alone: Texts and Reflections on Religious Experience,* trans. David L. Scheidt (Philadelphia: Fortress Press, 1978), p. 78.

29. Calvin, *Institutes,* III, IX, 5, pp. 717–18.

30. Edwards, *Thoughts,* p. 407.

31. Calvin, *Institutes,* III, VII, 6, p. 696.

32. Calvin, *Institutes,* III, XXI, 1, p. 922.

33. *Book of Confessions,* 7.036.

34. Charles Hodge, *The Way of Life and Selected Writings,* ed. Mark A. Noll (Mahwah, N.J.: Paulist Press, 1987), p. 223.

35. Calvin, *Devotions and Prayers of John Calvin,* ed. Charles E. Edwards (Grand Rapids: Baker Book House, 1954), p. 99.

7

The Discipline
of the Christian Life

Q. Since we are redeemed from our sin and its wretched consequences by grace through Christ without any merit of our own, why must we do good works?
A. Because just as Christ has redeemed us with his blood he also renews us through his Holy Spirit according to his own image, so that with our whole life we may show ourselves grateful to God for his goodness and that he may be glorified through us; and further, so that we ourselves may be assured of our faith by its fruits and by our reverent behavior may win our neighbors to Christ.

The Heidelberg Catechism[1]

The Christian life is not a matter of simply trusting in Christ and having everything work out as we want it to. The Reformed tradition has never tried to simplify the complexities and ambiguities that continue to plague the Christian throughout life. In spite of our wish that it might be otherwise, we are not exempted from the suffering, perplexity, and doubt common to all people. Calvin puts it very bluntly: "For whomever the Lord has adopted and deemed worthy of his fellowship ought to prepare themselves for a hard, toilsome, and unquiet life, crammed with very many and various kinds of evil."[2] We are not immune from the human situation. Christian faith does not exempt anyone from the tragedies of existence, which test the spirit. No matter how hard we pray or how deep our faith, we continue to be subject to troubles.

There are people who believe what they may call "the simple gospel." By this they mean that by believing hard enough a person can get wonderful blessings while avoiding the experiences of pain or disappointment. Such promises of escape from adversity almost always produce terrible pain and deep disappointment. People end up blaming themselves if things do not work out the way they want. The person was not healed, the marriage was not salvaged, the child was not saved because there was a deficiency of some kind in the believer. One feels that the person seeking the blessing did not have sufficient faith, or there was an unacknowledged sin in the person's life that blocked the work of the Spirit.

The cross is a central metaphor for the Christian life. Not only are we subject to the troubles of the rest of humanity, but there is a special suffering that goes with the voluntary taking up of our crosses as disciples of the Crucified One. To take up one's cross means more than to bear the pains that afflict all people. There is nothing voluntary in most human suffering; it happens to us. But there is another kind of suffering, which we take upon ourselves in the name of Jesus and as his disciples. Calvin called bearing the cross a central form of self-denial, and thus a necessary focus for Christian obedience. Christians are people who take up their own crosses. Yet this kind of self-denial is not simply an exercise in pain and misery. Calvin declares that there is often unexpected blessing in cross-bearing. "How much can it do to soften all the bitterness of the cross, that the more we are afflicted with adversities, the more surely our fellowship with Christ is confirmed! By communion with him the very sufferings themselves not only become blessed to us but also help much in promoting our salvation."[3]

In spite of the spiritual benefits of undeserved suffering, it is not easy to bear one's cross. Whether the troubles come to us from without as a curse from which we cannot flee or as a voluntary exercise of Christian obedience, they are really shattering. Bearing them may contain blessing, but the blessing is only to be found in the midst of the agony and tears. It is the injustice of so much human suffering that makes it so difficult to bear. Even though we may know with our minds that suffering is part of the disciple's life, we are never really prepared for it, and when it comes to us we often feel abandoned by God.

In contrast to the attitude of many contemporary Christians who create a sharp distinction between life before conversion and the new life in Christ that is free of doubts and troubles, the Reformed tradition insists that even the converted continue to suffer from these torments. And over against the attitude of some of liberal Protestantism that Christian growth in faith means steady improvement, the Reformed tradition insists that the struggle does not get easier, that growth in grace toward perfection has ups and downs, which keeps us humble. In the midst of his own personal troubles, Samuel Rutherford wrote, "I thought it had been an easy thing to be a Christian, and that to seek God had been at the next door, but O the windings, the turnings, the ups and the downs that He hath led me through!"[4]

The discipline of the cross is one that tests our love of the world's gifts and our aspiration for something of higher value, our faithfulness to God. Calvin emphasizes the centrality of adversity as God's way to wean us from excessive love of this life, using these events "to draw us back and to shake off our sluggishness, lest we cleave too tenaciously to that love."[5] He also stresses that we should not despise this life. "Since, therefore, this life serves us in understanding God's goodness, should we despise it as if it had no grain of good in itself? We must, then, become so disposed and minded that we count it among those gifts of divine generosity which are not at all to be rejected."[6] If we come to see this life as of less importance than the life to come, we may err by rejecting this world and its gifts. When we suffer as believers, we are torn between a sense of our own grief and a willingness to trust in God's grace. There are no easy answers.

A central affirmation that Calvin makes about the problem of the Christian life is that of inner contradiction. Believers are torn "between their natural sense, which flees and dreads what it feels adverse to itself, and their disposition to godliness, which even through these difficulties presses toward obedience to the divine will."[7] The struggle between honest admission of our own fears and reluctance to make sacrifices on the one hand, and our desire to be faithful to Christ on the other hand, is one that continues throughout life.

Because the Christian life is so difficult, and because the ambiguities are so great, the temptation toward easy answers is also great. We would all like to have life proceed at a smoother pace than it does. We would all prefer to have God be more clear and more unambiguous about what is expected of us. We all wish, at times at least, that God were more obviously present to us in the midst of our confusions and doubts.

Because faithfulness to God is so difficult, God's people have sought to respond to the question "How is it possible to live in the world and yet be faithful to God?" This has never been an easy question to answer. Every culture shapes its people in ways far beyond their consciousness. A certain amount of accommodation to one's culture is probably inevitable in order to survive in that culture. Yet, the people of God need to retain an identity that is different from that of their culture. If they are to have the inner resources that can enable them to bear witness within their culture, then they need to be, in some way, a peculiar people. Their ability to retain some marks of their faith will determine whether or not they can grow in their faith and live in obedience to the God in whom they profess belief.

The Christian life must have some shape, some central way of expressing itself. If left to chance, Christians are likely to be carried away by the latest cultural fad, or lulled into compromise with some form of idolatry. Without some clear priorities to provide guidance, we easily fall into a pattern of responding to crises as they come, or making priorities of whatever demands our attention the loudest.

When that becomes true for us, time for God gets squeezed out in the press of responsibility for a host of other people and things. The shape of the Christian life is its piety or spirituality. Only through the careful self-discipline and the nurturing strength of the community of faith are Christians enabled to establish and sustain a spirituality rooted and grounded in faith. The spiritual life is one that requires constant practice if it is not to degenerate into religion that is little more than duty.

In the Old Testament, a primary function of the law was to protect the people of the covenant from being absorbed by the alien cultures of the nations around them. The holiness code of Leviticus makes this very clear. "You shall not do as they do in the land of Egypt, where you lived, and you shall not do as they do in the land of Canaan, to which I am bringing you. You shall not follow their statutes. My ordinances you shall observe and my statutes you shall keep, following them: I am the Lord your God" (Lev. 18:3–4). Dozens of large and small activities performed daily exercised a powerful influence on the Israelite people. They knew who they were! Israel existed in a distinct and radical separation from other people, and its life was shaped by patterns carefully designed to protect it from being swallowed up by the practices of other people. The law accomplished that purpose well. In spite of the fact that the Hebrew people were a small, relatively insignificant nation set in the midst of mighty world powers, dispersed throughout many different nations, they have survived and preserved their identity in alien societies.

The New Testament church was concerned about this same problem. Its corporate life was shaped so that it stood out in the midst of its culture, not so much by what it did not do as by the positive nature of its corporate life. Luke describes the church in Acts: "The whole group of those who believed were of one heart and soul, and no one claimed private ownership of any possessions, but everything they owned was held in common. With great power the apostles gave their testimony to the resurrection of the Lord Jesus, and great grace was upon them all" (Acts

4:32–33). Here was a community that stood out in a world of greed, religious cynicism, and a terrible disparity between the few rich elite and the great masses of the poor, whether slave or free. Although there are many complex explanations, the Christian faith can be said to have won the soul of the Roman Empire because it offered a new vision of life. It presented a new way of being in the world, in which people mattered, in which there was mutual love and care, in which there was something worth living and dying for.

Ever since that time, Christians have struggled in different ways to come to terms with the fact that being disciples of Jesus involves both the need to let go of some things that culture tells us we must have and, at the same time, putting on certain practices that enable us to be clear about who we are in relationship to God. The disciplines of stripping away nonessentials and of assuming regular practices of the spiritual life are both important parts of maintaining a living and vital spirituality. The life of the spirit is expressed and nurtured by both of these dimensions. What we believe is shaped by our actions, and our actions are an expression of what we believe.

In the struggle to decide how to establish an identifiable pattern for their lives, Christians have taken very different paths. Some Christians have followed the lead of Tertullian, who in the third century A.D. declared many activities totally wrong for Christians, such as the theater, because of its origins in pagan worship practices; the dance, because it might arouse sexual passions; and cosmetics, because they produced an undue sense of pride. After the Constantinian legalization had made Christianity a political force of the Empire, many sensitive Christians retreated into the world of the monastic communities, where they could be relatively free from worldly temptation and devote themselves to prayer and the spiritual life. Most Christians who have continued to live in the world have been forced to struggle with the issue of how much to accommodate to the various cultures in which they have found themselves and how much they must protect themselves from enculturation by following a distinctive way of life. The tension between these two poles has been with the church ever since. Those Christians who have sought to keep themselves distinct and separate have been seen as overly scrupulous and rigid, while those who have accommodated to culture have been accused of "selling out" to the ways of the world.

Throughout his ministry, Calvin sought to make Geneva a city in which people expressed their faith by their behavior, a city in which righteousness could prevail. It was never easy—it cost him friends and reputation—but he was absolutely persuaded that the Christian could not dispense with the law, except at the peril of damnation. When received in freedom, the law of God could provide a basis for spiritual integrity. It could enable Christians to be nourished in a piety that could guide them through the dangers of life and provide assistance in the perplexities of temptation. Our obedience to the law is part of our freely given gratitude for what God has done for us. The law assists us in our weakness by guiding us as we seek to be faithful to the God whom we know as our Redeemer.

Although the Reformed tradition has frequently crossed over the line from using obedience to the law as part of Christian freedom to making obedience into a form of legalism, respect for the use of the law as a guide to conscience provides a necessary corrective on what could otherwise be life without restraint or limits. Without the aid of the law we may be left without any assistance as we try to make significant decisions.

Our Puritan forebears tried to come to terms with the problems of identity and purity in their own way. They lived as a minority in a social order in which royalty and privilege were established, and in which there was great wealth concentrated in the hands of a few. Puritans resisted what they perceived to be the dangers of wealth, of pomp and ceremony. They stressed the need for a way of life that avoided these excesses. They were faithful disciples of Calvin, sharing his concern to live prudently and carefully

in this world and resisting the desire for endless possessions, which must be kept in check in order to prevent it
from controlling everything.

In response to their situation, the Puritans became
adamantly opposed to any activity that participated in the
wealth and excessive display of the royal court. Thus they
forbade dance, the theater, cosmetics, and jewelry as well as
gambling. They also came to despise the excessive display
of wealth associated with the celebration of Christmas.
They were serious about the need to avoid getting caught up
in the love of money and in the greed and injustice against
which they protested.

The dangers they faced were many. There was a tendency
among them to be unduly proud of their morality and thus
harsh in their judgment of those who did not measure up to
their particular standards. The fault of the Puritans was
certainly not in their commitment, but their ambitious
search for purity led them to be overly concerned with
rejection of culture. They set out to organize a society of
redeemed and saintly human beings, restoring God's order
broken by the Fall. In their zeal, however, they forgot the
frailty of human nature; they forgot the ease with which
people can justify their own failures while condemning the
faults of others, and they forgot that standards of purity and
morality can be lived up to only if they are freely agreed
upon by the people themselves. They sought to impose
their values on a whole society, made up of people who did
not share their commitments and were reluctant to be
ordered about by Puritan moral standards. Puritans unfortunately became known for their judgmentalism, moralism,
and self-righteousness.

The dangers of Puritanism were exaggerated by nineteenth-century Protestants who became even more concerned about clearly defining the ways by which Christians
would be recognized and identified in the wider society.
They created lists of forbidden activities, and although the
specifics on the lists varied greatly from one denomination
to another and from one ethnic group to another, there was

a fairly set pattern of common taboos designed to show that a person took Christian faith seriously. In addition to the Puritan taboos about jewelry, cosmetics, dance, theater, and gambling, they added the use of tobacco and alcohol. They went so far as to redefine temperance as total abstinence, and so replaced Communion wine with grape juice. This horrified many conservatives, who believed that grape juice was an insult to Jesus and a transgression of scripture. In later times, attendance at motion pictures was added to the list of forbidden activities and, during the revivals of Charles Finney, drinking coffee and tea was included.

In reaction to these excesses of judgmentalism, self-righteousness, and rigidity, much of American Protestantism has vigorously rejected the whole notion of taboos. Even among conservative Protestants, use of the list has declined. Some of the strictest groups have tried to maintain the rejection of theater, but this is very difficult to do without hypocrisy when people have television sets in their own homes about which they gather to watch what they are forbidden to watch elsewhere. Most Protestants, despite feeling somewhat guilty, have accepted the pattern of conspicious consumption in our society without question. Except for attendance at church on Sunday mornings, it is often impossible to tell Christians apart from the rest of society by any external standard.

An urgent question that we all still face today is how we shape the pattern of our living so that there is something that holds together our belief and our practice. It is not enough to become obsessed about those things we do not do. Such an obsession has led to the self-righteousness and harsh judgmentalism to which we react with negativism and which we seek to avoid in ourselves.

We are shaped by what we do even more than by what we do not do. Our actions determine the kinds of persons we are more than we may choose to believe. Some form of discipline is an essential quality of the Christian life. Although he was writing about prayer, the truth of what Calvin wrote applies to the whole of life: "Our weakness is such that it has to be supported by many aids, and our sluggishness such that it needs to be goaded."[8] Unless we are committed to some kind of discipline, we are not likely to discover that we are growing in faith. A personal pattern of prayer that is meaningful does not develop by itself; it is the fruit of a commitment to regular times for prayer.

It is the discipline that we take on ourselves more than the discipline of removing something from our lives that may most determine our spirituality. In the nineteenth century a fairly common list of religious acts considered central was: (1) reading the Bible, (2) fasting, (3) keeping the Sabbath, (4) prayer, (5) almsgiving, and (6) doing works of charity and mercy. A more recent twentieth-century list would probably include the following: (1) moral living, including breaking bad habits, (2) prayer and private devotion, (3) the use of devotional literature, including the Bible as daily reading, (4) regular church attendance, and (5) service to others, including both witnessing and acts of charity and love.

Although grace is a gift, which is always freely given, we determine how we will respond to that gift. The Christian life is shaped by our response. Henry Scougal, the Scottish church leader, in his influential guide for the spiritual life, *The Life of God in the Soul of Man,* speaks about the role we must play in response to God's freely given grace. He says:

> We must break up our fallow ground, and root out the weeds, and pull up the thorns, that so we may be more ready to receive the seeds of grace and the dew of heaven. It is true, God hath been found of some who sought him not; he hath cast himself in their way, who were quite out of his; he hath laid hold upon them, and stopped their course of a sudden. . . . But certainly this is not God's ordinary method. . . . Though he [God] hath not tied himself to means, yet he hath tied us to the use of them.[9]

Discipline in the Christian life is not a luxury. Without it we become confused, lose our way, compromise our principles, and discover that we are not the people we had intended to be. No one is so sturdy in the faith that the temptation to surrender bit by bit does not erode conviction. Days go by and we discover that, instead of growing in grace in these days, we have wasted them.

These "means" to whose use we are tied, in Scougal's writing, are a positive set of directions for the Christian life, often called the "means of grace." The familiar vow once used when people united with the church was the promise to make diligent use of the means of grace. These means of grace are not a method of deserving God's grace, but a pattern by which we enable ourselves to be receptive to grace and remove the barriers that God permits us to erect as the price of our freedom. These tools, or aids, are ways by which we open ourselves to God's free grace. In using them, we shape our lives in order to become open to God's presence. They give our Christian pilgrimage a definite shape, in an age in which there is a general sense of loss of direction and confusion about right and wrong, along with an accompanying sense of God's absence.

The regular exercise of the means of grace is a good way to keep ourselves from being completely dominated by the culture around us. The regular and disciplined use of these means protects us from cultural captivity by shaping our minds, educating our wills, and forming our spirits. Baxter recommends a disciplined life which uses these means of grace "to prevent a shyness between God and thy soul. Frequent society breeds familiarity, and familiarity increases love and delight and makes us bold in our addresses. The chief end of this duty is to have acquaintance and fellowship with God, and therefore if thou come but seldom to it, thou wilt keep thyself a stranger still."[10] Calvin appreciated the means of grace as God's provision for our weakness. He writes that the purpose of them all is "that we may be united to God."[11]

The Public Means of Grace

Four of the most important means of grace have already been discussed: prayer, Bible-reading, consultation with others, and ethical living. These four are always exercised both privately and corporately. The private exercise of these means of grace is essential, but not sufficient for their greatest benefit. It would be impossible to engage in spiritual guidance without another person, at least on occasion, just as it would be impossible to engage in ethical living without dealing with other people. Yet each of these four means of grace involves the self in isolation also: One prays alone as well as in a community; one reads the Bible alone as well as in public worship; one must prepare for spiritual guidance alone before sharing with another person; one must resolve, in private, to take up a particular cause or champion a particular person or group. There are other means of grace which can be exercised only corporately; they always involve us with other people.

Worship

The first of the public means of grace is worship in the Christian community. As we participate in worship we open ourselves to the leading of God's Holy Spirit. Gathering with other believers to praise God, to hear God's Word read and interpreted, to pray, and to offer our lives in dedication to God's service, we are letting down our barriers to God. We consciously expose ourselves to the strength of the corporate community of faith. We subject ourselves to the power of encouragement that we receive from others and to the presence of God in the Word, spoken, preached, sung, and enacted in the sacraments.

Throughout the Reformed tradition, preaching has been understood as the vehicle by which the real presence of Christ is revealed and sealed among Christ's people in a way that is effective. In order for this spiritual benefit to take place, it is the responsibility of those who attend the Word to prepare to hear so that they may receive the word for them and practice it in their lives. A sense of expectancy may be the single most important quality necessary for the hearers to receive blessing from the preached Word.

Hearing a sermon is not a production dependent on the

preacher alone, but an event in which all present have a role. In a society such as ours, in which we are accustomed to being entertained as passive receivers, it is very difficult to participate in the preaching event. Whenever the preached Word is truly received by the hearer, the results are miraculous. Baxter attests to the power of the preached word: "What delights have I also found in the word preached? When I have sat under a heavenly, heart-searching teacher, how hath my heart been warmed? . . . How often have I gone to the congregation troubled in spirit and returned joyful? How often have I gone doubting, and God hath sent me home persuaded of his love in Christ?"[12]

The singing of hymns, which is central in Reformed worship, is a means by which we collectively offer praise and thanksgiving to God. Our hymnal is the prayer book of the Reformed church. Our hymns are, at their best, prayers that have the added benefit of being set to music. The music reinforces the power of the words, is an aid to memory, and assists the whole people to offer their worship together. As we join our voices with those of other believers, we are strengthened in faith and nurtured for the tasks of the week.

Worship does not always seem like a means of grace. There are, for us all, Sundays when the service simply does not touch us. We may be preoccupied with our own problems of family or work or health, or it may be that the service was constructed too narrowly around a theme that simply was not appropriate to our need. For example, a service of thanksgiving and praise may be completely inappropriate for someone who has just experienced the tragic death of a loved one. But there are other times, and they take place frequently enough to keep us returning, when we experience a lively sense of the presence of God and are touched by that presence. The experience may come through a hymn, an anthem, a prayer, or the sermon. Something about ourselves is illuminated, and we sense that in some mysterious way that particular element in the service was intended for us. We were directly and personally addressed through it.

The discipline of worship establishes a rhythm to life.

The pattern of examining our lives with others in the family of faith is important for our spiritual development. We have the opportunity each week to be addressed by scripture and to be supported and upheld by those around us who share our faith and also share our struggles to try to live faithfully. This community keeps us from a loss of identity. It helps us keep the channels in ourselves open to God. It assists us in remembering the sacred story in the midst of the incessant noise of other stories, and to apply it to our lives.

Sacraments

The second public means of grace is the sacraments. They deserve a special place in Reformed spirituality. It is no accident that all the confessional documents of the Reformed tradition give considerable attention to the sacraments. The Heidelberg Catechism, speaking of the manner in which faith originates, says: "The Holy Spirit creates it in our hearts by the preaching of the holy gospel, and confirms it by the use of the holy Sacraments."[13] This confirmation of faith is necessary for us amid the uncertainties and doubts into which we are cast, and gives the sacraments an essential role in our spiritual lives.

Because the baptism of infants has been normative for Reformed churches, they have tended to neglect the power of baptism as a means of grace. All too often it has become a charming ceremony of thanksgiving for the gift of a new life, a time to chuckle with delight at the antics of the child and to admire the parents, but not an awesome event in the faith journey of the whole congregation. Baptismal fonts are tiny objects dwarfed by pulpits and Communion tables. Baptism takes place in the service of worship at the most convenient time for the parents of a potentially noisy baby. The ritual is over quickly, and is treated as a private ceremony for the parents at which the congregation happens to be present as observer.

Yet every baptism is an occasion for proclaiming the

grace of God. As a little child is held, washed, sealed, and welcomed into the household of faith, each individual present is reminded that all of us are welcomed by the grace of God, not by anything that we have done to merit that acceptance. Calvin insists that because our baptism has washed us from sin for our whole life, the proper response is one of gratitude. "Therefore, as often as we fall away, we ought to recall the memory of our baptism and fortify our mind with it, that we may always be sure and confident of the forgiveness of sins."[14] Every time we witness a baptism we are reminded of the grace of God, which has been extended to include us. Thus every baptism is an opportunity for strengthening our faith.

The Lord's Supper is another occasion for deepening our faith, because in the eating and drinking we encounter the living Christ. Calvin believed, with no hesitation, that Christ was truly present in the holy meal. He summarized his argument in these words: "Our souls are fed by the flesh and blood of Christ in the same way that bread and wine keep and sustain physical life. For the analogy of the sign applies only if souls find their nourishment in Christ—which cannot happen unless Christ truly grows into one with us, and refreshes us by the eating of his flesh and the drinking of his blood."[15] In the sacrament we are united with Christ in mystical union.

Thus the sacrament is a primary means by which we are renewed in faith and sustained for faithfulness. The Heidelberg Catechism captures this high view of the sacrament in these words:

> Q. What does it mean to eat the crucified body of Christ and to drink his shed blood?
> A. It is not only to embrace with a trusting heart the whole passion and death of Christ, and by it to receive the forgiveness of sins and eternal life. In addition, it is to be so united more and more to his blessed body by the Holy Spirit dwelling both in Christ and in us that, although he is in heaven and we are on earth, we are nevertheless flesh of his flesh and bone of his bone, always living and being governed

by one Spirit, as the members of our bodies are governed by one soul.[16]

Each person who has ever participated in the sacrament of Holy Communion knows that there is a special sense of the Divine presence in the action of the breaking of the bread and pouring of the wine. We do something tangible, and in the action we are made aware of our relationship to Christ in a way that may be more concrete than at other times. Even though most Reformed congregations have forgotten Calvin's plea for weekly celebration and are more likely to celebrate the sacrament on a quarterly or monthly basis, it can still be said that sacramental mysticism remains a central means by which the spirituality of Reformed Protestants is sustained. A serious effort to reclaim the power of the sacraments today may have as much to do with a proper recovery of Reformed spirituality as any other action.

Participation in the Life of the Church

The third public means of grace is the regular participation of each of us in the fellowship of the life and mission of the church. This is more than attending worship on Sundays. It is the way in which we involve ourselves in the duties and responsibilities of church membership throughout the week. This is a means of grace, even though there are many times when it may seem more like a tiresome duty or burden. There are certainly occasions when the very act of hanging in when the church is torn by dissension and conflict is a painful discipline. It would be easier to forget the whole business and go about trying to live the Christian life by ourselves, without having to deal with all the problems that are always present when we are in relationship with other people.

Putting up with other Christians who disturb us or annoy us, or whose actions hurt us, is always unpleasant. Yet it can become a way in which we experience faith coming alive in trial. Jesus makes it clear throughout the Gospels that the life of the disciple is one that is to be shaped by the life of the Master. As we participate in the pain and struggle of discipleship, we discover his companionship.

Church involvement requires something from us. We are stretched beyond our self-imposed limits by taking upon ourselves responsibilities for work we otherwise might think we were not capable of doing. As we assume a particular duty with all the burdens that go with it, we often discover something important about ourselves. For example: The person who finally says yes to the persistent plea to teach a church school class after years of making excuses may discover that the experience itself is one that brings with it a new appreciation of the faith. The process of preparing lessons and of seeking to relate the faith to others is one in which the teacher grows toward deeper understanding of the faith. In the course of onerous duty, breakthroughs occur, and God's grace is discovered in fresh ways by the person who fulfills this duty.

Whenever we do something we fear we cannot do, we also discover that we have gifts we had not recognized before. We discover that in the performance of our responsibilities, we gain self-knowledge.

Giving

The fourth public means of grace is giving to others. When we part with something of value to us, whether it is our time, energy, or possessions, because someone else needs what we have to offer, we discover that grace is present in the very act of sharing. When we are willing to let go of something, we make ourselves vulnerable to God's grace. We get clarity about what really matters for us.

Sacrifices made on behalf of others are ways in which we model our lives after the Lord, who was always "for others." These acts put us in his company. As we reach out to give, especially when we do so without thought of what we are going to receive in return, we are the recipients of grace. If our giving is in expectation of getting something back, even the gratitude of the receiver, we may discover emptiness and bitterness rather than grace. Letting go with no strings attached is itself a way of making ourselves open to God's presence. If we seek reward, whether recognition or praise or gratitude, we may get nothing more as our reward. Our attitude is crucial.

Some people can seem very generous, yet use that generosity as a source of their pride. Outward actions and inward motivations can be very different. Calvin addresses the difference between outer behavior that appears to be motivated by love and genuine acts of love: "For it can happen that one who indeed discharges to the full all his obligations as far as outward duties are concerned is still all the while far away from the true way of discharging them."[17]

To experience blessing and grace in giving, we must let go of the gift with no strings attached. It is then that the promise of Jesus is that we shall receive much. The truth is difficult to grasp, because as long as we want to receive from our giving we will not receive. It is only when we are led to expect nothing that we shall be inwardly satisfied and experience blessing.

Our money is a symbol of ourselves. When we share our substance we are sharing our life with others. Our money represents time and energy, and these are the stuff of life itself. Those who receive from giving are united with us in a common bond, whether they are known to us or not. Giving stretches us and expands our horizons, especially when we give to a cause far from home. We cannot remain indifferent to the needs of those to whom we have given. The gift becomes a bond that opens us to concern for people around the world.

The key to giving as a means of grace is to be found in three necessary forms which that giving must take: (1) It must be giving without any strings attached, without any thought of reward or appreciation. That often means anonymous giving, for it is almost impossible to keep out the idea of gratitude when our giving is done for those who know us and know what we are doing for them. (2) Giving must be truly sacrificial. It must cause us to reexamine our priorities because it forces us to do without something important to us. Otherwise, giving can become only a way of making us feel good, of self-congratulation. Giving must demand something. The very act of making a sacrifice is a way of discovering the presence of God. Jesus made this very clear, saying: "As you did it to one of the least of these . . . you did it to me," and conversely, "As you did not do it to one of the least of these, you did not do it to me" (Matt. 25:40, 45). The companionship of Christ is discovered in the act of sacrifice. (3) Our giving must be accompanied by prayer. Both intercessory prayer and gifts of time and money are ways in which we allow the concerns and needs of others to become part of our consciousness.

Keeping the Sabbath

The fifth means of grace is keeping the Sabbath. Until the beginning of the twentieth century, the practice of a discipline of setting aside one day in seven was central to Reformed spirituality. The Sabbath was a day of rest from ordinary labor and special devotion to God. Rest from labor is only the beginning of keeping the Sabbath. Rest clears the way for positive activities which are otherwise difficult to make time for in our hectic lives. We are to use the time wisely in worship, recreation, reading, conversation, and enjoyment of friends and family, so that we are renewed and enabled to take up the responsibilities of life with more vigor and enthusiasm.

Over the centuries, Reformed observance of the Sabbath became harsh, rigid, and legalistic. It became a burden, which demanded that all people avoid certain practices and perform others. Bayly lists all those things from which Christians are to refrain on the Sabbath:

> First, from all the works of our calling. . . . Secondly, From carrying burdens, as carriers do; or riding abroad for profit, or for pleasure. . . . Thirdly, from keeping of fairs, or

markets. . . . Fourthly, from studying any books of science, but the holy Scriptures and Divinity. . . . Fifthly, from all recreations and sports. . . . Sixthly, from gross feeding, liberal drinking of wine, or strong drink; which may make us either drowsy or unapt to serve God with our hearts and minds. Seventhly, from all talking about worldly things, which hindereth the sanctifying of the Sabbath, more than working.[18]

This is, indeed, a severe regimen, and one that became intolerable for most people despite threats of divine punishment or social ostracism.

Our rebellion against Sabbath legislation has succeeded almost totally. Our use of the large amount of discretionary time available to us today, with Monday holidays and long weekends, does not seem to be able to refresh us. Our practice of Sabbath rest is probably inferior to that of our ancestors in spite of our freedom from their bondage to laws. We exhaust ourselves in activity and are worn out at the conclusion of what should have been time for renewal and rest. Why else is Monday the most difficult and exhausting day of the whole week?

Calvin addressed the purpose of Sabbath-keeping in a more positive way, to demonstrate that it could serve as an aid for the spiritual life. He suggested three reasons for keeping Sabbath: First, to use it as a time for meditating upon the final Sabbath rest at the end of life, so that God can work in us through the Spirit; second, so that we can meditate upon God's works in our lives; and third, so that we do not oppress those who work for us.[19] Each of these three reasons for Sabbath observance deserves fresh thought in our time.

We have flattened time so that every day is like every other, and there is no balance between work and leisure and certainly little time left for devotion to God and to deeds of charity and mercy. Our eagerness to do and to get have overwhelmed us to the point that we are prisoners to the clock and the labor we perform. Sabbath, whether one day in seven or in some other pattern, is an important reminder to us of the importance of rest, of the centrality of paying attention to God, of the centrality of public worship, and of the need to be mindful of the needs of others who also need rest.

All these corporate means of grace are necessary for us. We cannot dispense with any of them. Along with the more private means of grace (prayer, meditation on scripture, and spiritual guidance), they enable us to shape our lives in response to God's graciousness toward us. They can, of course, become a new legalism, a way of binding the conscience and of producing the smug, self-satisfied attitude that destroyed the framework of Puritan piety. But each of the means of grace can also be a way in which we are made more ready to become faithful as God chooses to lead us. We need to be careful not to make any discipline into a new law, but we also need to be careful that we do not reject all guidance and try to live by what feels right in the moment.

Unless we understand that the means of grace are gifts, they can become burdens, and we shall discover that we berate ourselves for not living up to our own expectations. We are often more severe with ourselves than God's graciousness to us should permit. Our use of the means of grace is not for the purpose of satisfying God, but for the renewal of our lives. We do not have to achieve some standard of perfection in order for them to be helpful for us. Calvin reminds us, "Sons . . . do not hesitate to offer [their fathers] incomplete and half-done and even defective works, trusting that their obedience and readiness of mind will be accepted."[20]

Jesus said that he came that we might have life and have it more abundantly. The spiritual life, the pursuit of God's presence, the longing for a personal relationship with God are a human response to the divine invitation. These are never something we do on our own. It is God's prompting that initiates the spiritual pilgrimage. God wills the good for each of us and offers a life that is rewarding and filled with vitality, but we cannot have this on our own. It is in relationship with God that we discover something that cannot be had in any other way. Contrary to popular misunderstanding, the opposite of spiritual is not physical, but lifeless, dull, and monotonous. To be spiritual is to be filled with vigor for life, to be enthusiastic about life, to really love life, and to dare to live deeply and fully.

The biblical promise that if we truly seek, we shall find God is the basis for the journey of the spiritual life. In spite of the difficulties along the way, the times of dryness when nothing seems to be happening, the discouragement and distraction that come to us all, and the times of falling back and wondering if we have made any progress at all, the journey is one from which we cannot turn back. The testimony of the saints of all the ages is that the journey is worth it; that God really is love; and that the love God offers is the most important reality that can be known by any of us. Such knowledge enables a person to have tremendous power to take what happens, to surmount great difficulties, and to grow in the face of tragedy and deep disappointment.

The fruit of the spiritual life is not easily attained. The process of growing in grace is sometimes difficult. It requires persistence which never comes easily for any of us. The old part of us, the part that wants to go it alone and maintain control, keeps asserting itself. There are times when we want to go back to being unaware and half dead. God requires honesty from us, and such honesty can be painful. Because God knows us better than we know ourselves, pretending will not work. God's knowledge of us demands that we come to terms with who we really are.

In a beautiful summary of the process of growth in grace, Flora Wuellner says this: "As we are healed and pulled together into wholeness, we are shown many things that we had not seen before. We are shown feelings we have had, but which have been repressed. We are shown things we have done, judgments we have made during our days of blindness and insensitivity. We are shown relationships in a new light, and facts to which we had not awakened. And as we wake and see, decisions about what we see begin to rise in freshness and power."[21]

The goal of the Christian life is union with Christ, but such union is only dimly and occasionally realized in this life by most of us. Nevertheless, the pilgrimage toward the goal is one of joyful discovery that Christ is with us whether or not we realize that presence. We are given new opportunities for relationship with others along the way. We find new possibilities within us that we had not thought possible. The adventure of the Christian life is one that demands all we can give it. But the testimony of the ages is that the goal of the adventure is well worth the struggle. The hungry heart of the pilgrim is fed along the way.

> Grant, Almighty God, that as nothing has been omitted by thee to help us onward in the course of our faith, and as our sloth is such that we hardly advance one step though stimulated by thee,—O grant that we may strive to profit more by the various helps which thou hast provided for us, so that the law, the prophets, the voice of John the Baptist, and especially the doctrine of thine only-begotten Son, may more fully awaken us, that we may not only hasten to him, but also proceed constantly in this course, and persevere in it until we shall at length obtain both the victory and the crown of our calling, as thou hast promised an eternal inheritance reserved in heaven for all who faint not, but wait for the coming of that great Redeemer. Amen.
>
> John Calvin[22]

NOTES

1. Presbyterian Church (U.S.A.), *Book of Confessions* (New York and Atlanta: Office of the General Assembly, 1983), 4.086.

2. John Calvin, *Institutes of the Christian Religion,* ed. John T. McNeill, trans. Ford Lewis Battles (Philadelphia: Westminster Press, 1960), III, VIII, 1, p. 702.

3. Calvin, *Institutes,* p. 702.

4. Samuel Rutherford, *Religious Letters* (Edinburgh and London: Anderson & Ferrier, 1894), p. 216.

5. Calvin, *Institutes,* III, IX, 1, p. 712.

6. Calvin, *Institutes,* III, IX, 3, p. 715.

7. Calvin, *Institutes,* III, VIII, 10, p. 710.

8. Calvin, *Institutes,* III, XX, 50, p. 917.

9. Henry Scougal, *The Life of God in the Soul of Man,* ed. Winthrop S. Hudson (Philadelphia: Westminster Press, 1948), p. 68.

10. Richard Baxter, *The Saints' Everlasting Rest* (New York: Doubleday & Co., 1978), p. 134.

11. John Calvin, *Commentaries: The Book of Psalms,* trans. James Anderson (Grand Rapids: Baker Book House, 1984), 24:7–8, vol. 1, p. 410.

12. Baxter, *Saints' Everlasting Rest,* p. 164.

13. *Book of Confessions,* 4.065.

14. Calvin, *Institutes,* IV, XV, 3, p. 1305.

15. Calvin, *Institutes,* IV, XVII, 10, p. 1370.

16. *Book of Confessions,* 4.076.

17. Calvin, *Institutes,* III, VII, 7, p. 697.

18. Lewis Bayly, *The Practice of Piety* (London: Daniel Midwinter, 1714), pp. 252–55.

19. Calvin, *Institutes,* II, VIII, 34, p. 400.

20. Calvin, *Institutes,* III, XIX, 5, p. 837.

21. Flora Slosson Wuellner, *On the Road to Spiritual Wholeness* (Nashville: Abingdon Press, 1978), p. 57.

22. Calvin, *Devotions and Prayers of John Calvin,* ed. Charles E. Edwards (Grand Rapids: Baker Book House, 1954), p. 117.

Bibliography:
Reformed Spirituality

Ames, William. *Conscience, with the Power and Cases Thereof.* Translated for Publique Benefit. London: 1643. Reprint, Norwood, N.J.: Walter J. Johnson, Inc., 1975.

Augustine of Hippo. *The Confessions of Saint Augustine.* Translated by Edward B. Pusey. New York: Random House, Modern Library, 1949.

Baillie, John. *A Diary of Private Prayer.* New York: Charles Scribner's Sons, 1955.

Barbour, G. F. *The Life of Alexander Whyte, 1836–1926.* London: Hodder & Stoughton, 1923.

Barth, Karl. *Prayer: According to the Catechisms of the Reformation.* Stenographic Records of Three Seminars. Adapted by A. Roulin. Translated by Sara F. Terrien. Philadelphia: Westminster Press, 1952.

Battles, Ford Lewis, trans. *The Piety of John Calvin.* Grand Rapids: Baker Book House, 1973.

Baxter, Richard. *A Call to the Unconverted.* Grand Rapids: Baker Book House, 1976. Reprint of edition published for the American Tract Society, New York, 1835.

———. *Converse with God in Desertion and Solitude.* Philadelphia: Presbyterian Board of Publication, n.d.

———. *The Reformed Pastor.* New York: Robert Carter & Brothers, 1860. Original publication, 1656.

———. *The Saints' Everlasting Rest.* Doubleday & Co., 1978. In *The Doubleday Devotional Classics,* edited by Glenn Hinson, vol. 1. Garden City, N.Y.: Doubleday & Co., 1978. Original publication, 1647.

Bayly, Lewis. *The Practice of Piety.* London: Printed for Daniel Midwinter, at the Three Crowns, in St. Paul's Church-yard, 1714. Original publication, c. 1610.

Bell, Richard H. *Sensing the Spirit.* Philadelphia: Westminster Press, 1984.

Benner, David G. *Psychotherapy and the Spiritual Quest.* Grand Rapids: Baker Book House, 1987.

Bloesch, Donald G. "A Christological Hermeneutic: Crisis and Conflict in Hermeneutics." In *The Use of the Bible in Theology: Evangelical Options,* edited by Robert K. Johnston. Atlanta: John Knox Press, 1985.

————. *The Struggle of Prayer.* San Francisco: Harper & Row, 1981.

Boesak, Allan, and Charles Villa-Vicencio, eds. *When Prayer Makes News.* Philadelphia: Westminster Press, 1986.

Bonar, Horatius. *Bible Thoughts and Themes.* New York: Robert Carter & Brothers, 1890.

Bonhoeffer, Dietrich. *Spiritual Care.* Translated by Jay C. Rochelle. Philadelphia: Fortress Press, 1985.

————. *The Way to Freedom: Lectures and Notes 1935–1939.* Vol. 2 of *The Collected Works of Dietrich Bonhoeffer.* Edited by Edwin H. Robertson. Translated by Edwin H. Robertson and John Bowden. London: William Collins Sons & Co., 1966.

Borchert, Gerald L., and Andrew D. Lester, eds. *Spiritual Dimensions of Pastoral Care: Witness to the Ministry of Wayne E. Oates.* Philadelphia: Westminster Press, 1985.

Bouwsma, William. *John Calvin: A Sixteenth-Century Portrait.* New York: Oxford University Press, 1987.

————. "The Spirituality of John Calvin." In *Christian Spirituality: High Middle Ages and Reformation.* Vol. 17 of *World Spirituality: An Encyclopedic History of the Religious Quest,* edited by Jill Raitt, Bernard McGinn, and John Meyendorff. New York: Crossroad, 1987.

Bouyer, Louis. *Orthodox Spirituality and Protestant and Anglican Spirituality: A History of Christian Spirituality II.* New York: Seabury Press, 1969.

Bradstreet, Anne. *The Works of Anne Bradstreet in Prose and Verse.* Edited by John Ellis. Charlestown, Mass., 1867. Reprint, Gloucester, Mass.: Peter Smith, 1962.

Brainerd, David. *Diary.* Edited by Jonathan Edwards. Vol. 2 of The Doubleday Devotional Classics. Garden City, N.Y.: Doubleday & Co., 1978.

Brauer, Jerald C., "Puritan Mysticism and the Development of Liberalism." *Church History* (September 1950).

Brown, Robert McAfee, *Creative Dislocation: The Movement of Grace.* Nashville: Abingdon Press, 1980. A volume in the Journeys in Faith series, edited by Robert A. Raines.

———. *Reading the Bible Through Third World Eyes.* Philadelphia: Westminster Press, 1984.

———. *Spirituality and Liberation.* Philadelphia: Westminster Press, 1988.

Bruce, Robert. *The Mystery of the Lord's Supper.* London: James Clarke & Co., 1958.

Brueggemann, Walter. *The Creative Word.* Philadelphia: Fortress Press, 1982.

———. *Praying the Psalms.* Winona, Minn.: St. Mary's Press, 1982.

Buechner, Frederick: *The Final Beast.* San Francisco: Harper & Row, 1982.

———. *Now and Then.* San Francisco: Harper & Row, 1983.

———. *A Room Called Remember: Uncollected Pieces.* San Francisco: Harper & Row, 1984.

———. *The Sacred Journey.* San Francisco: Harper & Row, 1982.

Bunyan, John. *Grace Abounding to the Chief of Sinners.* In *The Doubleday Devotional Classics,* edited by Glenn Hinson, vol. 1. Garden City, N.Y.: Doubleday & Co., 1978.

———. *I Will Pray with the Spirit.* Edited by Richard L. Greaves. Oxford: Clarendon Press, 1976.

———. *Pilgrim's Progress.* In *The Doubleday Devotional Classics,* edited by Glenn Hinson, vol. 1. Garden City, N.Y.: Doubleday & Co., 1978.

Bushnell, Horace. *Sermons.* Edited by Conrad Cherry. In *Sources of American Spirituality.* Mahwah, N.J.: Paulist Press, 1985.

Buttrick, George Arthur. *Prayer.* Nashville: Abingdon-Cokesbury Press, 1942.

———. *So We Believe, So We Pray.* Nashville: Abingdon-Cokesbury Press, 1951.

Caldwell, Patricia. *The Puritan Conversion Narrative.* New York: Cambridge University Press, 1983.

Calvin, John. *Calvin: Theological Treatises.* Translated by J. K. S. Reid. Philadelphia: Westminster Press, 1954.

———. *Commentaries: The Book of Daniel.* 2 vols. Translated by Thomas Myers. Grand Rapids: Baker Book House, 1984.

———. *Commentaries: The Book of Ezekiel.* Translated by

Thomas Myers. Grand Rapids: Wm. B. Eerdmans Publishing Co., 1948.

―――. *Commentaries: The Book of Psalms.* Vols. 1 and 2. Translated by James Anderson. Grand Rapids: Baker Book House, 1984.

―――. *Commentaries on the Catholic Epistles.* Translated and edited by John Owen. Grand Rapids: Baker Book House, 1984.

―――. *Commentaries on the Epistles of Paul to the Galatians and Ephesians.* Translated by William Pringle. Grand Rapids: Baker Book House, 1984.

―――. *Commentaries on the First Book of Moses Called Genesis.* Vols. 1 and 2. Translated by John King. Grand Rapids: Wm. B. Eerdmans Publishing Co., 1984.

―――. *Commentary on a Harmony of the Evangelists.* Vols. 1, 2, 3, and 4. Translated by William Pringle. Grand Rapids: Wm. B. Eerdmans Publishing Co., 1949.

―――. *Commentary on the Book of the Prophet Isaiah.* Translated by William Pringle. 2 vols. Grand Rapids: Baker Book House, 1984.

―――. *Commentary on the Epistles of Paul the Apostle to the Corinthians.* Vols. 1 and 2. Translated by John Pringle. Grand Rapids: Wm. B. Eerdmans Publishing Co., 1948.

―――. *Commentary on the Four Last Books of Moses.* Vols. 1, 2, and 3. Translated by Charles W. Bingham. Grand Rapids: Baker Book House, 1843.

―――. *Devotions and Prayers of John Calvin.* Edited by Charles E. Edwards. Grand Rapids: Baker Book House, 1954.

―――. *The Epistles of Paul the Apostle to the Romans and to the Thessalonians.* Translated by Ross Mackenzie. Grand Rapids: Wm. B. Eerdmans Publishing Co., 1961.

―――. *Institutes of the Christian Religion.* Edited by John T. McNeill. Translated by Ford Lewis Battles. Philadelphia: Westminster Press, 1960.

―――. *The Letters of John Calvin.* 4 vols. Compiled by Jules Bonnet. Translated by David Constable and M. R. Gilchrist. Philadelphia: Presbyterian Board of Publication, n.d.

Campbell, Alastair. *Rediscovering Pastoral Care.* Philadelphia: Westminster Press, 1981.

Carter, Harold A. *The Prayer Tradition of Black People.* Valley Forge, Pa.: Judson Press, 1976.

Cheyne, A. C., ed. *The Practical and the Pious: Essays on Thomas Chalmers.* Edinburgh: Saint Andrew Press, 1985.

Coburn, John. *Prayer and Personal Religion.* Philadelphia: Westminster Press, 1957.

Cohen, Charles Lloyd. *God's Caress: The Psychology of Puritan Religious Experience.* New York: Oxford University Press, 1986.

Cott, Nancy F. *The Bonds of Womanhood: Women's Sphere in New England, 1780–1835.* New Haven, Conn.: Yale University Press, 1977.

Dabney, Robert L. *Discussions: Evangelical and Theological.* Vols. 1 and 2. London: Banner of Truth Trust, 1967.

Dent, Arthur. *The Plaine Mans Pathway to Heaven.* London: Robert Dexter, 1629. First edition, 1601.

Dillenberger, John, and Claude Welch. *Protestant Christianity: Interpreted Through Its Development.* New York: Charles Scribner's Sons, 1954.

Dod, John. *A Plain and Familiar Exposition on the Lord's Prayer.* 2nd edition. London, 1635.

Doddridge, Philip. *The Rise and Progress of Religion in the Soul.* Philadelphia, 1843. Original publication, 1745.

———. *Sermons to Young People.* London: Hartford, 1803.

Dodds, Elisabeth D. *Marriage to a Difficult Man: The "Uncommon Union" of Jonathan and Sarah Edwards,* Philadelphia: Westminster Press, 1971.

Douglass, Jane Dempsey. *Women, Freedom, and Calvin.* Philadelphia: Westminster Press, 1985.

Dowey, Edward A. *The Knowledge of God in Calvin's Theology.* New York: Columbia University Press, 1952.

Downame, John. *A Guide to Godlyness, or a Treatise of a Christian Life.* London, 1622.

Dyrness, William A. "How Does the Bible Function in the Christian Life?" In *The Use of the Bible in Theology: Evangelical Options,* edited by Robert K. Johnson. Atlanta: John Knox Press, 1985.

Edwards, Jonathan. "Thoughts on the Revival of Religion in New England, 1742." In *Edwards on Revivals.* New York: Dunning & Spaulding, 1832.

———. *Religious Affections.* Edited by John E. Smith. Vol. 2 of *The Works of Jonathan Edwards.* New Haven, Conn.: Yale University Press, 1959.

Edwards, Tilden. *Living in the Presence: Disciplines for the Spiritual Heart.* San Francisco: Harper & Row, 1986.

———. *Sabbath Time: Understanding and Practice for Contemporary Christians.* New York: Seabury Press, 1982.

———. *Spiritual Friend: Reclaiming the Gift of Spiritual Direction.* New York: Paulist Press, 1980.

Ellul, Jacques. *Prayer and Modern Man.* New York: Seabury Press, 1970.

Erskine, Thomas. *Letters of Thomas Erskine of Linlathen.* Edited by William Hanna. Edinburgh: Clark, 1877.

Fairchild, Roy. *Finding Hope Again.* San Francisco: Harper & Row, 1980.

———. "Spiritual Direction in Pastoral Care: Guaranteed Not to Shrink." *Pacific Theological Review* 16, no. 1 (Fall 1982).

Farley, Edward. *Requiem for a Lost Piety.* Philadelphia: Westminster Press, 1956.

Ferguson, Duncan S. *Biblical Hermeneutics: An Introduction.* Atlanta: John Knox Press, 1986.

Flavel, John. *The Mystery of Providence.* London: Banner of Truth Trust, 1963. Original publication, 1678.

———. *A Saint Indeed.* Amherst, N.H.: Coverly, 1795. American Antiquarian Society. Microfilm. Originally published in 1671.

Forstman, H. Jackson. *Word and Spirit: Calvin's Doctrine of Biblical Authority.* Stanford, Calif.: Stanford University Press, 1962.

Forsyth, Peter T. *The Soul of Prayer.* London: Independent Press, 1916.

Fosdick, Harry Emerson. *The Meaning of Prayer.* New York: Follett Publishing Co., 1949.

Foster, Richard. *Celebration of Discipline: The Path to Spiritual Growth.* San Francisco: Harper & Row, 1978.

———. *Freedom of Simplicity.* San Francisco: Harper & Row, 1981.

Fox, George. *The Journal of George Fox.* Garden City, N.Y.: Doubleday & Co., 1978.

Fremantle, Anne. *The Protestant Mystics.* Boston: Little, Brown & Co., 1964.

Gerrish, Brian A. *The Old Protestantism and the New.* Chicago: University of Chicago Press, 1982.

Gibble, Kenneth. "Listening to My Life: An Interview with Frederick Buechner." *The Christian Century* (March 1988).

Glaser, Chris. *Come Home! Reclaiming Spirituality and Community as Gay Men and Lesbians.* San Francisco: Harper & Row, 1990.

Goodwin, Thomas. *The Collected Works,* Vols. 1–5. Edinburgh: James Nichol & Co., 1861.

———. *The Work of the Holy Spirit in Our Salvation.* Carlisle, Pa.: Banner of Truth Trust, 1980.

Hageman, Howard G. "Reformed Spirituality." In *Protestant Spiritual Traditions,* edited by Frank C. Senn. New York: Paulist Press, 1986.

Hall, David D. *The Faithful Shepherd: A History of the New England Ministry in the Seventeenth Century.* Chapel Hill, N.C.: University of North Carolina Press, 1973.

Hambrick-Stowe, Charles. *Early New England Poetry: Anne Bradstreet and Edmond Taylor.* New York: Paulist Press, 1987.

———. *The Practice of Piety: Puritan Devotional Disciplines in Seventeenth-Century New England.* Chapel Hill, N.C.: University of North Carolina Press, 1982.

Harbaugh, Henry. *The Heavenly Home; or, The Employments and Enjoyments of the Saints in Heaven.* Philadelphia: Lindsay & Blakiston, 1853.

Harding, M. Esther. *Journey Into Self.* New York, Longmans, Green & Co. 1956.

Harkness, Georgia. *The Dark Night of the Soul.* Nashville: Abingdon-Cokesbury Press, 1945.

———. *The Fellowship of the Holy Spirit.* Nashville: Abingdon Press, 1966.

———. *John Calvin: The Man and His Ethics.* New York: Henry Holt & Co., 1931.

———. *Mysticism: Its Meaning and Message.* Nashville: Abingdon Press, 1973.

———. *Prayer and the Common Life.* Nashville: Abingdon-Cokesbury Press, 1948.

Haroutunian, Joseph, ed. *Calvin: Commentaries.* Philadelphia: Westminster Press, 1979.

Hastings, James. *The Doctrine of Prayer.* Edinburgh: T. & T. Clark, 1915.

Hatch, Nathan O., and Harry S. Stout. *Jonathan Edwards and the American Experience,* New York: Oxford University Press, 1988.

Henry, Matthew. *A Method of Prayer.* Philadelphia: Presbyterian Board of Publication, n.d.

Herbert, George. *The Country Parson and The Temple.* Edited and with an introduction by John Nelson Wall. From The Classics of Western Spirituality series. Mahwah, N.J.: Paulist Press, 1986.

Herman, Emily. *Creative Prayer.* New York: Harper & Brothers, 1934.

———. *The Finding of the Cross.* New York: George H. Doran, 1926.

———. *The Meaning and Value of Mysticism.* New York: George H. Doran, 1925.

———. *The Touch of God.* New York: George H. Doran, 1926.

Heyer, George S., Jr. "Prayer in the Reformed Tradition." Austin Seminary *Bulletin* 101, no. 4 (October 1985).

Hinson, Glenn. "Puritan Spirituality." In *Protestant Spiritual Traditions,* edited by Frank C. Senn. New York: Paulist Press, 1986.

Hodge, Charles. "Conference Papers." In *Charles Hodge: Selected Writings,* edited by Mark Noll. New York: Paulist Press, 1987.

———. *The Way of Life and Selected Writings.* Edited by Mark A. Noll. In Sources of American Spirituality series. Mahwah, N.J.: Paulist Press, 1987.

Holifield, E. Brooks. *The Covenant Seals: The Development of Puritan Sacramental Theology in Old and New England, 1570–1720,* New Haven, Conn.: Yale University Press, 1974.

———. *A History of Pastoral Care in America.* Nashville: Abingdon Press, 1983.

Holmes, Urban T. *A History of Christian Spirituality.* New York: Seabury Press, 1980.

———. *Spirituality for Ministry.* San Francisco: Harper & Row, 1982.

Jansen, John Frederick. *Calvin's Doctrine of the Work of Christ.* London: James Clarke & Co., 1952.

Jensen, Peter F. "Prayer in a Reformed Perspective." *Reformed Theological Review,* September–December, 1987.

Johnson, Ben Campbell. *Pastoral Spirituality: A Focus for Ministry.* Philadelphia: Westminster Press, 1988.

———. *To Pray God's Will: Continuing the Journey.* Philadelphia: Westminster Press, 1987.

———. *To Will God's Will: Beginning the Journey.* Philadelphia: Westminster Press, 1987.

Jones, Alan. *Exploring Spiritual Direction: An Essay on Christian Friendship.* New York: Seabury Press, 1982.

———. *Journey Into Christ.* New York: Seabury Press, 1972.

Jones, E. Stanley. *Growing Spiritually.* Nashville: Abingdon-Cokesbury Press, 1953.

Jones, Rufus. *Spiritual Reformers in the 16th and 17th Centuries.* Boston: Beacon Press, 1959.

Jones, W. Paul. *The Province Beyond the River: The Diary of a Protestant at a Trappist Monastery.* New York: Paulist Press, 1981.

Kang, Young Woo. *A Light in My Heart.* Atlanta: John Knox Press, 1987.

Kaufman, U. Milo. *The Pilgrim's Progress and Traditions in Puritan Meditation.* New Haven, Conn.: Yale University Press, 1966.

Kelly, Thomas R. *A Testament of Devotion,* New York: Harper & Brothers, 1941.

Kelsey, David H. *The Uses of Scripture in Recent Theology.* Philadelphia: Fortress Press, 1975.

Kelsey, Morton. *Adventure Inward.* Minneapolis: Augsburg Publishing House, 1980.

———. *Caring: How Can We Love One Another?* New York: Paulist Press, 1981.

———. *Christo-Psychology.* New York: Crossroad, 1982.

———. *Companions on the Inner Way: The Art of Spiritual Guidance.* New York: Crossroad, 1983.

———. *Discernment: A Study in Ecstasy and Evil.* New York: Paulist Press, 1978.

———. *Dreams: A Way to Listen to God.* New York: Paulist Press, 1978.

———. *Healing and Christianity.* New York: Harper & Row, 1976.

———. *The Other Side of Silence: A Guide to Christian Meditation.* New York: Paulist Press, 1976.

———. *Reaching: The Journey to Fulfillment.* San Francisco: Harper & Row, 1989.

———. *Resurrection: Release from Oppression.* New York: Paulist Press, 1985.

———. *Tongue Speaking: An Experiment in Spiritual Experience.* Garden City, N.Y.: Doubleday & Co., 1964.

———. *Transcend: A Guide to the Spiritual Quest.* New York: Crossroad, 1981.

King, Martin Luther, Jr. *Strength to Love.* In *A Martin Luther King Treasury.* Negro Heritage Library. Yonkers, N.Y.: Educational Heritage, 1964.

Knox, Ronald A. *Enthusiasm.* London: Oxford University Press, 1950.

Laing, David, ed. *The Works of John Knox.* Vols. 1–6. Edinburgh: Thomas George Stevenson, 1864.

Lake, Peter. *Anglicans and Puritans? Presbyterianism and English Conformist Thought from Whitgift to Hooker.* Boston: Unwin & Hyman, 1988.

Laubach, Frank. *Channels of Spiritual Power.* Westwood, N.J.: Fleming H. Revell Co., 1954.

———. *Prayer, the Mightiest Force in the World.* Westwood, N.J.: Fleming H. Revell Co., 1959.

Law, William. *A Serious Call to a Devout and Holy Life.* Edited by Paul G. Stanwood. New York: Paulist Press, 1978.

Leech, Kenneth. *Soul Friend: The Practice of Christian Spirituality.* San Francisco: Harper & Row, 1977.

———. *True Prayer.* San Francisco: Harper & Row, 1980.

Leith, John H. *An Introduction to the Reformed Tradition.* Atlanta: John Knox Press, 1977.

———. *John Calvin's Doctrine of the Christian Life.* Louisville, Ky.: Westminster/John Knox Press, 1989.

Leonard, Bill J., ed. *Becoming Christian: Dimensions of Spiritual Formation.* Louisville, Ky.: Westminster/John Knox Press, 1990.

Lewis, C. S. *Letters to Malcolm: Chiefly on Prayer.* New York: Harcourt, Brace & World, 1964.

———. *The Screwtape Letters.* New York: Macmillan Co., 1943.

Loder, James. *The Transforming Moment: Understanding Convictional Experiences.* New York: Harper & Row, 1981.

Lovelace, Richard. *Dynamics of Spiritual Life.* Downers Grove, Ill.: Inter-Varsity Press, 1979.

Mather, Cotton. *Diary of Cotton Mather.* Edited by Worthington Chauncey Ford. New York: Frederick Ungar Publishing Co., 1957. Original publication, 1911.

May, Gerald G. *Care of Mind—Care of Spirit: Psychiatric Dimensions of Spiritual Direction.* San Francisco: Harper & Row, 1982.

———. *Will and Spirit: A Contemplative Psychology.* San Francisco: Harper & Row, 1982.

McGiffert, Michael, ed. *God's Plot: The Paradoxes of Puritan Piety, Being the Autobiography and Journal of Thomas Shepherd.* Amherst, Mass.: University of Massachusetts Press, 1972.

McNeill, John T. *A History of the Cure of Souls.* New York: Harper & Brothers, 1951.

———. *The History and Character of Calvinism.* New York: Oxford University Press, 1954.

Miller, Perry. *The New England Mind: The Seventeenth Century.* Boston: Beacon Press, 1954. Original publication, 1939.

Miller, Thomas E. "A Recovery of Social Piety." Montreat, N.C.: Montreat Management Council, Montreat Conference Center, 1987.

Mitchel, Jonathan. *Discourse of the Glory.* London: J. Collins, 1677. Appendix to the 2d edition, "A Letter to His Friend."

Mollenkott, Virginia Ramey. *Speech, Silence, Action.* Nashville: Abingdon Press, 1980.

Moltmann, Jürgen. *Experiences of God.* Translated by Margaret Kohl. Philadelphia: Fortress Press, 1980.

Moremen, William. *Developing Spiritually and Professionally.* Philadelphia: Westminster Press, 1984.

Mulholland, M. Robert, Jr. *Shaped by the Word: The Power of Scripture in Spiritual Formation.* Nashville: Upper Room, 1985.

Nelson, James B. *Between Two Gardens: Reflections on Sexuality and Religious Experience.* New York: Pilgrim Press, 1983.

Niebuhr, H. Richard. *The Meaning of Revelation.* New York: Macmillan Co., 1941.

Nouwen, Henri J. M. *Reaching Out: The Three Movements of the Spiritual Life.* Garden City, N.Y.: Doubleday & Co., 1975.

Nuttall, Geoffrey F. *The Holy Spirit in Puritan Faith and Experience.* Oxford: Basil Blackwell, 1946.

Oates, Wayne. *Nurturing Silence in a Noisy Heart.* Garden City, N.Y.: Doubleday & Co., 1979.

———. *The Christian Pastor.* Philadelphia: Westminster Press, 1981.

O'Connor, Elizabeth. *Call to Commitment.* New York: Harper & Row, 1963.

———. *Journey Inward, Journey Outward.* New York: Harper & Row, 1968.

———. *Search for Silence.* Waco, Tex.: Word, 1972.

Old, Hughes Oliphant. *The Patristic Roots of Reformed Worship.* Zurich: Theologischer Verlag, 1975.

———. *Praying with the Bible.* Philadelphia: Geneva Press, 1980.

———. *Worship That Is Reformed According to Scripture.* Atlanta: John Knox Press, 1984.

Oliver, Fay Conlee. *Christian Growth Through Meditation.* Valley Forge, Pa.: Judson Press, 1976.

O'Malley, J. Stevens. *Pilgrimage of Faith: The Legacy of the Otterbeins.* Metuchen, N.J.: Scarecrow Press, 1973.

Osterhaven, M. Eugene. *The Spirit of the Reformed Tradition.* Grand Rapids: Wm. B. Eerdmans Publishing Co., 1971.

Owen, John. *The Glory of Christ.* Edited by Wilbur M. Smith. Chicago: Moody Press, 1949.

―――. *Sin and Temptation.* Abridged and edited by James M. Houston. Portland, Ore.: Multnomah Press, 1983.

Palmer, Parker J. *The Active Life: A Spirituality of Work, Creativity and Caring,* San Francisco: Harper & Row, 1990.

Pannenberg, Wolfhart. *Christian Spirituality.* Philadelphia: Westminster Press, 1983.

Parker, T. H. L. *Calvin's New Testament Commentaries.* Grand Rapids: Wm. B. Eerdmans Publishing Co., 1971.

―――. *The Doctrine of the Knowledge of God: A Study in the Theology of John Calvin.* Edinburgh: Oliver and Boyd, 1952.

―――. *John Calvin: A Biography.* Philadelphia: Westminster Press, 1975.

―――. *The Oracles of God: An Introduction to the Preaching of John Calvin.* London: Lutterworth Press, 1947.

Perkins, William. *The Whole Treatise of the Cases of Conscience . . . Taught and Delivered by M. W. Perkins in His Holy-Day Lectures.* London: T. Pickering, 1611.

Peterson, Eugene H. *A Long Obedience in the Same Direction.* Downers Grove, Ill.: Inter-Varsity Press, 1980.

―――. *Working the Angles: The Shape of Pastoral Integrity.* Grand Rapids: Wm. B. Eerdmans Publishing Co., 1987.

Petit, Norman. *The Heart Prepared: Grace and Conversion in Puritan Spiritual Life.* New Haven, Conn: Yale University Press, 1966.

Phelps, Austin. *The Still Hour.* Boston: Gould & Lincoln, 1860.

Porterfield, Amanda. *Feminine Spirituality in America from Sarah Edwards to Martha Graham.* Philadelphia: Temple University Press, 1980.

Postema, Don. *Space for God.* Grand Rapids: Christian Reformed Church Publications, 1983.

Potter, G. R. *Huldrych Zwingli.* New York: St. Martins Press, 1977.

Presbyterian Church (U.S.A.). *The Constitution of the Presbyterian Church (U.S.A.), Part I, The Book of Confessions.* New York and Atlanta: Office of the General Assembly, 1983. Part II, *The Book of Order*. Louisville, Ky.: Office of the General Assembly, 1990.

Preston, John. *The Saint's Daily Exercise: A Treatise Unfolding the Whole Duty of Religion*. 3d edition. London, 1629.

Pruyser, Paul W. *The Minister as Diagnostician*. Philadelphia: Westminster Press, 1976.

Raitt, Jill, ed. *Christian Spirituality*. Vol. 17 of *World Spirituality: An Encyclopedic History of the Religious Quest*. New York: Crossroad, 1988.

Rauschenbusch, Walter. *Selected Writings*. Edited by Winthrop S. Hudson. In *Sources of American Spirituality*. Mahwah, N.J.: Paulist Press, 1986.

Reynolds, Edward. *A Treatise of the Passions and Faculties of the Soule of Man, with the severall Dignities and Corruptions thereunto Belonging*. London, 1640.

Rice, Howard L. "Feasting and Fasting in the Reformed Tradition." *Pacific Theological Review* 22 (Fall 1988).

Richard, Lucien Joseph. *The Spirituality of John Calvin*. Atlanta: John Knox Press, 1974.

Rinker, Rosalind. *Communicating Love Through Prayer*. Grand Rapids: Zondervan Publishing House, 1966.

Roberts, Robert C. "What Is Spirituality?" *Reformed Journal* 33 (August 1987).

Rogers, Jack. *Presbyterian Creeds: A Guide to the Book of Confessions*. Philadelphia: Westminster Press, 1985.

Rogers, Jack, and Donald K. McKim. *The Authority and Interpretation of the Bible,* San Francisco: Harper & Row, 1979.

Rous, Francis. "The Mystical Marriage." *Treatises and Meditations*. London: Robert White, 1657.

Rowe, Elizabeth Singer. *Devout Exercises of the Heart*. Edited by Isaac Watts. Baltimore: J. Kingston, 1811. Original publication, 1737.

———. *Friendship in Death,* 3rd edition. London: T. Worrall, at Judge Coke's Head Against St. Dunstan's Church in Fleet Street, 1733.

———. *Letters Moral and Entertaining*. Part I, 1728; Part II, 1731; and Part III, 1732. Reprinted, with an introduction by Josephine Grieder. New York: Garland Publishing Co., 1972.

Rutherford, Samuel. *Religious Letters*. Edinburgh and London: Anderson & Ferrier, 1894.

———. *The Tryall and Triumph of Faith*. London, 1645.

Ryken, Leland. *Worldly Saints: The Puritans as They Really Were.* San Diego: Academie Books, 1986.

Saliers, Don E. *Worship and Spirituality.* Philadelphia: Westminster Press, 1984.

Sanford, Agnes. *The Creation Waits.* Los Angeles: Bridge Publications, 1977.

———. *The Healing Light.* St. Paul: Macalester Park Publishing Co., 1968.

Sanford, John A. *Healing and Wholeness.* New York: Paulist Press, 1968.

———. *The Kingdom Within.* Philadelphia: J. B. Lippincott Co., 1970.

Schleiermacher, Friedrich. *The Christian Faith.* English translation of the 2d German ed.. Edited by H. R. Mackintosh and J. S. Stewart. Edinburgh: T. & T. Clark, 1928.

Schutz, Roger (Prior of Taizé). *The Rule of Taizé.* Taizé, France: Les Presses de Taizé, 1968.

Scougal, Henry. *The Life of God in the Soul of Man.* Edited by Winthrop S. Hudson. Philadelphia: Westminster Press, 1948.

Senn, Frank S., ed. *Protestant Spiritual Traditions.* Mahwah, N.J.: Paulist Press, 1974.

Shea, Daniel B., Jr. *Spiritual Autobiography in Early America.* Princeton, N.J.: Princeton University Press, 1968.

Sheldon, Charles M. *In His Steps.* Old Tappan, N.J.: Fleming H. Revell Co., Spire Books, 1963.

Shepherd, J. Barrie. *Praying the Psalms: Daily Meditations on Cherished Psalms.* San Francisco: Harper & Row, 1987.

Shepherd, Thomas. *The Works of Thomas Shepherd.* Edited by James Adams Albro. 3 vols, 1853. Reprint. New York: Georg Olms Verlag, 1971.

Shoemaker, Samuel. *By the Power of God.* New York: Harper & Brothers, 1954.

———. *The Experiment of Faith: A Handbook for Beginners.* New York: Harper & Brothers, 1957.

Sibbes, Richard. *The Complete Works of Richard Sibbes.* Nichol Series of Standard Divines, 1862.

Singh, Sadhu Sundar. *At the Master's Feet.* Translated by Arthur and Rebecca Parker. Madras, India: Christian Literature Society, 1957.

Soelle, Dorothee. *Death by Bread Alone: Texts and Reflections on Religious Experience.* Translated by David L. Scheidt. Philadelphia: Fortress Press, 1978.

———. *Suffering.* Translated by Everett R. Kalin. Philadelphia: Fortress Press, 1975.

Steere, Douglas. *Dimensions of Prayer.* New York: Board of Global Ministries of the United Methodist Church, 1962.

———. *On Beginning from Within.* New York: Harper & Brothers, 1943.

———. *On Listening to Another.* New York: Harper & Brothers, 1955.

Stendahl, Krister. *Paul Among Jews and Gentiles and Other Essays.* Philadelphia: Fortress Press, 1976.

Stevens, W. P. *The Holy Spirit in the Theology of Martin Bucer.* New York: Cambridge University Press, 1970.

Stoeffler, F. Ernest. *The Rise of Evangelical Pietism.* Leiden: E. J. Brill, 1965.

Stringfellow, William. *The Politics of Spirituality.* Philadelphia: Westminster Press, 1984.

Teellinck, William. *The Resting Place of the Mind, for All Afflicted Hearts. . . .* London: E. Brewster, 1622.

Tersteegen, Gerhard. *Spiritual Letters.* Translated and edited by Peter Erb. From *Pietists: Selected Writings.* New York: Paulist Press, 1983.

Thayer, Nelson S. T. *Spirituality and Pastoral Care.* Philadelphia: Fortress Press, 1985.

Thompson, Ernest Trice. *The Spirituality of the Church: A Distinctive Doctrine of the Presbyterian Church in the United States.* Richmond: John Knox Press, 1961.

Thurian, Max. *Modern Man and the Spiritual Life.* New York: Association Press, 1963.

Thurman, Howard. *The Centering Moment.* Richmond, Ind.: Friends United Press, 1971.

———. *Deep Is the Hunger.* New York: Harper & Brothers, 1951.

———. *Disciplines of the Spirit.* New York: Harper & Row, 1963.

———. *Jesus and the Disinherited.* Nashville: Abingdon-Cokesbury Press, 1949.

———. *With Head and Heart: The Autobiography of Howard Thurman.* New York: Harcourt Brace Jovanovich, 1979.

Toon, Peter. *From Mind to Heart: Christian Meditation Today.* Grand Rapids: Baker Book House, 1986.

Torrance, Thomas Forsyth. *Calvin's Doctrine of Man.* London: Lutterworth Press, 1952.

Tournier, Paul. *A Doctor's Casebook in the Light of the Bible.* New York: Harper & Row, 1960.

————. *Escape from Loneliness.* Translated by John S. Gilmour. Philadelphia: Westminster Press, 1962.

Trueblood, D. Elton. *The Company of the Committed.* New York: Harper & Row, 1961.

————. *The Essence of Spiritual Religion.* New York: Harper & Brothers, 1936.

Underhill, Evelyn. *The Letters of Evelyn Underhill.* Edited by Charles Williams. London: Longmans Green, 1943.

————. *Mysticism.* New York: E. P. Dutton & Co., Meridian Books, 1957.

————. *The Mystics of the Church.* New York: Attic Press, 1975.

————. *Worship.* New York: Crossroad, 1982.

Underwood, Ralph L. "The Presence of God in Pastoral Care." *Austin Seminary Bulletin* 101, no. 4 (October 1985).

United Presbyterian Church in the U.S.A. "Communal and Personal Prayer." The Advisory Council on Discipleship and Worship of the General Assembly. New York: Office of the General Assembly, 1980.

Vischer, Lucas. *Intercession.* World Council of Churches Faith and Order Paper No. 95. Geneva, 1980.

Wakefield, Gordon S. *Puritan Devotion: Its Place in the Development of Christian Piety.* London: Epworth Press, 1957.

————. *The Westminster Dictionary of Christian Spirituality.* Philadelphia: Westminster Press, 1983.

Walker, Henry. *Spiritual Experiences, Of Sundry Believers.* London, 1653.

Wallace, Ronald S. *Calvin's Doctrine of the Christian Life.* Grand Rapids: Wm. B. Eerdmans Publishing Co., 1959.

————. *Calvin's Doctrine of the Word and Sacrament.* Edinburgh: Oliver & Boyd, 1953.

————. *Christian Spirituality.* Indianapolis: Bobbs-Merrill Co., 1956.

Waller, George M., ed. *Puritanism in Early America.* Lexington, Mass.: D. C. Heath & Co., 1950.

Warfield, Benjamin B. *Calvin and Calvinism.* New York: Oxford University Press, 1931.

————. *Perfectionism.* Philadelphia: Presbyterian and Reformed Publishing Co., 1958.

Watson, John. *The Cure of Souls.* The Lyman Beecher Lectures on Preaching at Yale University. New York, 1896.

Weatherhead, Leslie D. *A Private House of Prayer.* Nashville: Abingdon Press, 1958.

Webbe, George, William Perkins, and Richard Rogers. *A Garden of Spiritual Flowers.* London: Published by Robert Bird at the Sign of the Bible in St. Catherine Lane, 1635. Microfilm.

Wells, David F. "The Nature and Function of Theology." In *The Use of the Bible in Theology: Evangelical Options,* edited by Robert K. Johnson. Atlanta: John Knox Press, 1985.

Wesler, Daniel B., and M. Jenelyn. *The Gifts of Silence.* Atlanta: John Knox Press, 1976.

Wesley, John. *Selected Writings.* Edited by Frank Whaling. New York: Paulist Press, 1981.

Whichcote, Benjamin. *Select Aphorisms.* Christian Tract Society, XXVIII. London: G. Smallfield, 1822.

White, Alexander. *The Teachings of Thomas Goodwin.* Edinburgh: Oliphants, n.d.

White, Elizabeth. *The Experiences of God's Gracious Dealing with Mrs. Elizabeth White.* Boston: S. Kneeland and T. Green, 1741.

White, Helen C. *English Devotional Literature, 1600–1640.* Madison, Wis.: University of Wisconsin Press, 1931.

White, John. *A Way to the Tree of Life: Discourses in Sundry Directions for the Profitable Reading of the Scriptures.* Preface by Thomas Goodwin. London: Published by M.F. for R. Royston, 1647.

Williams, Daniel Day. *The Minister and the Care of Souls.* New York: Harper & Row, 1961.

Willis, David. *Daring Prayer.* Atlanta: John Knox Press, 1977.

———. "Piety: Sound and Substance." *Pacific Theological Review* 6, no. 2 (Summer 1974).

———. "Reformed Piety and Consumer Pietism." *Reformed Liturgy and Music* 8, no. 4 (Summer 1974).

Wink, Walter. *The Bible in Human Transformation: Towards a New Paradigm for Biblical Study.* Philadelphia: Fortress Press, 1973.

———. *Transforming Bible Study: A Leader's Guide.* Nashville: Abingdon Press, 1980.

Wolterstorff, Nicholas. *Until Justice and Peace Embrace.* Grand Rapids: Wm. B. Eerdmans Publishing Co., 1983.

World Council of Churches. "Spirituality for Our Times." World Council Paper. Geneva, 1985.

Wuellner, Flora Slosson. *On the Road to Spiritual Wholeness.* Nashville: Abingdon Press, 1978.

———. *Prayer and the Living Christ.* Nashville: Abingdon Press, 1969.

——. *Prayer and Our Bodies.* Nashville: Upper Room, 1987.
——. *Prayer: Stress and Our Inner Wounds.* Nashville: Upper Room, 1985.
Wyon, Olive. *The School of Prayer.* London: Student Christian Movement Press, 1943.
Yrigoyen, Charles, and George H. Bricker, eds. *Catholic and Reformed: Theological Writings of John Williamson Nevin.* Pittsburgh: Pickwick Press, 1978.
Zwingli, Huldrych. "Of the Clarity and Certainty or Power of the Word of God." In *Zwingli and Bullinger,* edited by G. W. Bromiley. Vol. 24, Library of Christian Classics. Philadelphia: Westminster Press, 1953.

Index